PROSPEROUS
WICKED
and
PLAGUED
SAINTS

An Exposition of Psalm 73

David J. Engelsma

Reformed Free Publishing Association
Jenison, Michigan

Scripture cited is taken from the King James Version

Reformed Free Publishing Association
1894 Georgetown Center Drive
Jenison MI 49428-7137

Phone: 616-457-5970
Fax: 616-457-5980
Website: www.rfpa.org
E-mail: mail@rfpa.org

ISBN 978-0-916206-96-3
LCCN 2007827548

*To my colleagues and students
at the Protestant Reformed Seminary*

Contents

CONTENTS

Preface

Psalm 73 rescues every believing child of God from one of the most powerful and dangerous temptations with which he or she ever struggles. It is the temptation to doubt the favor of God because of the troubles of earthly life. The saints are plagued.

Lending force to this already strong temptation is the seeming favor of God to his unbelieving enemies in the circumstances of their earthly lives. The wicked prosper.

This alone makes a faithful exposition of Psalm 73 eminently worthwhile. God's people need the help of the word of God in Psalm 73. They needed it in the time of Old Testament Israel. They need it no less today.

But there is another reason why all Christians will benefit from an explanation and application of Psalm 73. The psalm exposes and demolishes the popular, prevalent error of a common grace of God: the teaching that the prosperity of the wicked is indeed God's favor to the wicked. Flying in the face of the instruction of Psalm 73, the teaching of common grace tends to destroy the struggling child of God in his grievous temptation. For if the prosperity of the wicked is grace, the troubles of the believer are divine disfavor. Common grace explicitly denies the secondary theme of Psalm 73: The prosperity of the wicked is nothing but "slippery places" unto

destruction. Common grace implicitly contradicts the main
theme of Psalm 73: "Truly God is good to Israel."

I am not aware of any commentary on Psalm 73 that does
justice to its purpose of comforting the godly concerning their
troubled earthly circumstances by allaying their fear that God
blesses the wicked in their present prosperity. Most commen-
taries do not even address the precise issue in the psalm. I am
certain that no defender of common grace dares to acknowledge Psalm 73, much less expound it.

The exposition in this book began as a series of exegetical,
devotional speeches to the students and professors at the Theological School of the Protestant Reformed Churches in the
weekly "chapel exercises." At the urging of both the students
and my colleagues, I have prepared this exposition for publi-
cation.

DAVID J. ENGELSMA
Professor of Old Testament and Dogmatics
Theological School of the Protestant Reformed Churches

Introduction

Psalm 73 was composed by Asaph, as the heading indicates. Asaph was a Levite. King David appointed Asaph as a minister of music, vocal and instrumental, in the public worship of God before the ark in Jerusalem (1 Chron. 15:16, 17, 19; 1 Chron. 16:4, 5, 7, 37; 1 Chron. 25:1, 2, 6, 7). David made the appointment on the occasion of the triumphal ascent of the ark to Jerusalem (1 Chron. 15, 16). A gifted musician, Asaph led the choir of singing Levites. He also accompanied the choir with cymbals: "Asaph made a sound with cymbals" (1 Chron. 16:5). Hundreds of years later, after the return of Judah from exile, Asaph's descendants were still fulfilling the musical office of their illustrious forebear (Ezra 2:41; Ezra 3:10; Neh. 7:44; Neh. 11:17, 22; Neh. 12:35, 36).

The songs were the inspired psalms. Asaph, who composed the music of the covenant people, as well as directed and accompanied it, wrote at least twelve psalms. One is found in Book 2 of the Psalms—Psalm 50. The other eleven, including Psalm 73, are included in Book 3—Psalms 73–83. A reading of these psalms shows that Asaph had a lively sense of the warfare of the people of God with the ungodly and a profound awareness of the suffering and struggles of the saints in this life.

The psalms are instructive. Unlike many hymns, and certainly unlike the mindless ditties with which much of contem-

porary evangelicalism amuses itself, the psalms are sound doctrine. Singing the psalms to the praise of God, the worshiping
congregation is taught. The doctrine of Psalm 73 is the good
news that God blesses his chosen people in all the circumstances of everyday, earthly life. Verse 1 proclaims this gospel:
"Truly God is good to Israel." The clear and necessary implication is that God does not bless the impenitently ungodly. This
is more than an implication of the teaching of Psalm 73. It is
the explicit doctrine of the psalm: "Thou didst set them in slippery places" (v. 18).

Psalm 73 settles the issue whether God, in favor, blesses the
ungodly in the good things of their earthly lives. This is a doctrinal issue. It is the issue of common grace. Common grace explains the prosperity of the wicked as God's blessing of the
wicked in a favor, or love, he has toward them in history. Not
only is the doctrine of a common grace of God the prevailing
opinion in the churches, but it is also a common assumption in
the world of the ungodly. Unbelieving men and women look
over their wealth and comfortable lives and say, "We are
blessed."

The issue whether God indeed blesses the ungodly is of
great practical importance to the man or woman who fears the
Lord. The issue arises in Psalm 73 in the form of an urgent,
practical question: "Does God indeed bless the ungodly, as
seems to be the case?" If he does, he also curses the godly in his
disfavor; for the godly, by contrast, suffer all kinds of adversities. And if this is true—if the prosperity of the wicked is divine blessing, necessarily implying that the adversity of the

righteous is divine curse—the effect upon the godly is spiritual destruction. Supposing that God blesses the wicked and curses the righteous had the effect upon the psalmist that his "feet were almost gone," that his "steps had well nigh slipped" (v. 2). This threatened spiritual falling, spiritual collapse, spiritual disaster.

If it is true, as is widely believed and taught, that God blesses the ungodly, the child of God will conclude, "I have cleansed my heart in vain, and washed my hands in innocency" (v. 13). This is spiritual despair.

From this despair the gospel of Psalm 73 rescues the Christian who is shaken to his spiritual foundations by the doubt that God may favor the ungodly. "Truly God is good to Israel" (v. 1).

CHAPTER ONE

Particular Goodness

*Truly God is good to Israel, even to such as are
of a clean heart* (Ps. 73:1).

Grace Regarding Things

THE great doctrinal issue whether God has a favor to the ungodly and a corresponding disfavor to the godly, with its important practical implications, is resolved by the truth of the goodness of God. The goodness of God in verse 1 is not the perfection of his glorious being. The psalmist was not tempted to doubt the goodness of God's being. Nor is God's goodness the general righteousness of all his dealings with his human creatures. In the sense of the righteousness of his dealings, God is good toward all humans without exception. He will be good in this sense toward the reprobate ungodly when he damns them.

But the goodness of God confessed in Psalm 73 is an attitude of favor toward men and women according to which he blesses them. God has a good disposition toward certain persons. He loves them. He is gracious toward them. He has a favorable attitude toward them.

In his goodness, God *does* good to these people. All his dealings with them are governed by his favor. In all he gives them and in all he withholds from them, he accomplishes their good. This is the subject of Psalm 73: God's favor, or grace, toward people so that he blesses them.

Particularly, the goodness of God is his favorable attitude toward, and his blessing of, people *regarding the circumstances of their earthly lives,* whether of prosperity or adversity, health or sickness, ease or distress. The goodness of verse 1 is not the blessings of the forgiveness of sins, holiness, and the hope of life eternal. This goodness, the psalmist was not tempted to doubt. But it is the favor that seems to be evident in the material prosperity of the ungodly (vv. 3–12). It is the blessing that the child of God has a hard time experiencing when he is plagued and chastened in his job and possessions, in his family, and in his health (v. 14).

Good to the Church

In precisely this sense of goodness, God is good to Israel. The object of God's goodness has the emphasis in the text according to the word order of the Hebrew text: "Truly good *to Israel* (is) God." This is the urgent question in Psalm 73, as in the experience of everyone who fears God: To whom is God good? Whom does he favor? Whom does he bless: Israel or the wicked?

The blessed object of the gracious goodness of God is Israel. Israel is the nation whom God has eternally elected in his love in Jesus Christ (Ex. 19:6; 1 Pet. 2:9). Israel is the people whom God has redeemed by the death of his own Son (Deut. 7:8; 1 Pet. 1:18, 19). Israel is the bride of God, with whom God has established his covenant in Christ so that he dwells with her in the intimacy of the real marriage (Ezek. 16; Eph. 5:22–33). Israel is the body of living members whom God renews and cleanses by his Holy Spirit. The holiness of the true Israel is prominent in the text: "to such as are of a clean heart."

Israel is the church.

Israel is the object of the divine goodness in the everyday, earthly lives of the members of the elect and holy nation. Regarding earthly things and circumstances, God has a favorable attitude toward Israel. In these earthly things and circumstances, God blesses Israel. In his providential government of the earthly lives of the citizens of Israel, God intends and accomplishes their welfare.

Only to Israel is God good. This is incontrovertibly the teaching of verse 1: To Israel is God good, *and to none else.* That the teaching of verse 1 is the exclusive goodness of God to Israel becomes immediately plain as soon as one tries to read the verse differently: "Truly good to Israel is God, *and also to the wicked.*" In addition, the exclusive goodness of God stands in the very nature of the case. If God is good to the wicked simply by virtue of the material prosperity he gives them, he is not good to the Israelite who not only lacks prosperity, but also suffers trouble and want. But this is a flat contradiction of the emphatic declaration of verse 1: "God is good to Israel." Besides, the argument of the psalm in the verses that follow contends that, although it seems God is good to the wicked, in fact he is not good to them—not at all.

The Wicked Excluded

God is not good to those who are not Israel. They are those persons who do not have a clean, that is a regenerated and sanctified, heart (v. 1). They are those who are "foolish" (v. 3); "wicked" (v. 3); proud and violent (v. 6); corrupt blasphemers of God and slanderers of God's people (vv. 8, 9); "ungodly" (v. 12); and far from God (v. 27).

The ungodly in Psalm 73, who are not Israel, are the reprobate wicked. They are those men and women whom God has eternally appointed to destruction. For them Christ did not die. With them God does not establish his covenant of friendship and salvation by the Spirit of Christ. This is evident in that these wicked persons finally perish everlastingly (vv. 18, 27). Psalm 73 draws an absolute contrast between elect Israel, who are saved everlastingly in the way of sanctification, and the reprobate wicked, who perish everlastingly on account of their own ungodliness.

There is reason to explain the ungodly and wicked of the psalm as primarily the reprobate wicked in the sphere of the covenant. In the language of the Old Testament, they are the many Israelites who, although they have outward membership in the nation, are not among the remnant who love, fear, worship, and serve God from the heart (Isa. 1:9). The apostle describes this remnant as the "remnant according to the election of grace"

(Rom. 11:5). In the terminology of the apostle Paul, these wicked are the persons who are merely "of Israel," but who are not God's "Israel" (Rom. 9:6).

The evidence in Psalm 73 that the wicked are the ungodly in the sphere of the covenant is, first, that their lives are always before the eyes of the psalmist. Verse 3 says that the psalmist saw the prosperity of the wicked. He would hardly be surveying the lives of Philistines and Edomites. Second, verse 27 describes them as people who go "a-whoring" from God. Spiritual adultery is the sin of those who transgress the covenant. Unfaithful members of the visible church play the whore by forsaking God for idols.

God is not good to these ungodly and wicked by having a favorable attitude toward them. He is not good to them by blessing them. He is not good to them in this life with regard to their comfortable circumstances and abundant possessions. With these circumstances and possessions, God neither intends nor accomplishes their welfare. If God is not good to the ungodly, he is wrathful toward them, so that he curses them.

Psalm 73 exposes as false the popular doctrine of common grace. This doctrine teaches that God blesses the reprobate ungodly *in this life, with regard to earthly gifts and physical circumstances,* such as rain and sunshine, riches, health, and family. God supposedly blesses the ungodly because he has a gracious, or loving, attitude toward them. Precisely in the sense that Psalm 73 declares, "Truly good to Israel is God," common grace says, "Truly God is good to the foolish, the wicked, the proud and violent, corrupt blasphemers of God and scoffers at the church, and those who have gone a-whoring from him." When common grace says this, it also necessarily says, "Truly God is not good to Israel." He will be good to Israel in the life hereafter, but he is not good to Israel here and now regarding the earthly circumstances of the lives of the clean of heart. For their earthly lives are plagued and chastened (v. 14).

Psalm 73 refutes the lie of common grace. It demolishes this theory. It is the purpose of the Holy Spirit with this psalm to deny the doctrine of common grace. The psalm exposes the error of common grace plainly and directly. The psalm does not deny that God gives many good earthly gifts to the ungodly, so that, as a rule, their lives are comfortable, pleasurable, and successful. On the contrary, the psalm affirms that this is the case. This is the problem for the God-fearing psalmist.

But the psalm denies that these gifts and these circumstances are God's blessing. By these material gifts and in these earthly circumstances, God is not good to the ungodly.

So much is it true that God's goodness is particular, not common, that the psalmist qualifies his statement that the object of God's goodness is Israel. The qualification is, "even to such as are of a clean heart." The Authorized Version captures the thought correctly: "even." We may understand the text this way: "God is good to Israel, that is, to the clean of heart." The qualification further defines Israel, as well as individualizes the objects of God's goodness. God is not good to all without exception who may outwardly belong to the nation of Israel in its historical manifestation. God is not good to all without exception who hold membership in the visible church. For not all of them are the true Israel of God. Some are merely "of Israel" (Rom. 9:6).

True Israelites are those who have a clean heart. They have been regenerated by the Holy Spirit. They are inwardly as well as outwardly separated from the foolish, ungodly, wicked world. They are consecrated to God in thankful love, so that they cleanse their hearts and wash their hands (v. 13).

To them, and to them only, God is gracious. Them, and them only, he blesses.

The Certainty of Goodness

His goodness to true Israelites is certain: "Truly." The word with which Psalm 73 begins is a small but expressive word. It expresses the certainty of the affirmation of verse 1, which is also the theme of the psalm. It is the Hebrew Old Testament equivalent of the Greek New Testament's "verily." Indeed, verse 13 of Psalm 73 translates this word "verily." There is absolutely no doubt about it: God is good to Israel.

The word translated "truly" expresses also that God is *only* good to Israel. Never is his attitude toward Israel that of hateful wrath. Never are his dealings with Israel those of curse.

In addition, the word expresses that the doctrine of God's goodness to Israel in earthly life is true, even though the circumstances of Israel's life seem to contradict the doctrine. The force of "truly" is this: "Notwithstanding the seeming blessing of the ungodly and notwithstanding the seeming disfavor of God to me in the hard circumstances of my earthly life, God is good to Israel, including me, and he is not good to the ungodly."

"Truly" expresses the certainty of faith, not of sight. As he freely confesses in the verses that follow, the psalmist did not always experience the truth of God's goodness to Israel and to himself. In fact, he doubted this goodness. In the way of a serious spiritual struggle, he had to learn God's goodness to him. But this does not imply that God's goodness to Israel is a truth that the psalmist arrives at only at the end of his struggle with doubt. Rather, it is his starting point. It is a fundamental truth of the gospel that he believes and confesses even though he does not experience it. On the basis of this undoubted truth, he struggles with his doubt, and struggles finally victoriously.

Goodness Revealed in the Cross

The truth that God blesses Israel—in this life regarding the earthly circumstances of life—is an essential doctrine of the gospel. God has promised to be good to his Israel. God has promised to be good, and good only. God has promised to be good to his Israel, not only in spiritual blessings, but also regarding the earthly circumstances of the lives of the members of Israel. God has revealed his gracious attitude toward his Israel in the cross of his Son. By that cross, God has averted all curse from Israel and made Israel the rightful object of his blessing. "He that spared not his own Son, but delivered him up for us all, how shall he not with him also freely give us all things?" (Rom. 8:32).

Although the goodness of God in Psalm 73 is not the perfection of his being but his gracious blessing of his people, the perfection of his being is at stake in the truth of the psalm. From the perfection of his being comes his goodness to his people. God's goodness to Israel reveals that God is good in himself. And if God is not in fact good to Israel in this life, but rather good to the ungodly, then he is not good in himself. He is not good because he has promised to be good to his people. A god who does not keep his promise is not the God of the gospel of Christ.

Likewise, the teaching that God blesses the reprobate ungodly is not an insignificant error. It is a mistake to suppose that theologians may endlessly debate the issue of common grace in a spirit of tolerance. The truth of the being and perfections of God are at stake. For example, God is a righteous God. As a righteous God, he blesses men and women in accordance with his own righteousness and on the ground of their righteousness through the atoning death of Jesus Christ. On what basis does God bless the ungodly, who are outside the elect church of Christ by God's own decree of reprobation? The only explanation by those who confess the biblical doctrine that Christ died only for the elect church is that God's grace ignores and conflicts with his righteousness. He has an attitude of favor, or love, toward men and women and blesses them apart from the cross of Christ. But if God can bless guilty sinners apart from the cross of Christ in earthly life and with regard to material things, why cannot he also extend his saving favor and the blessings of eternal life to them apart from the righteousness of the death of Christ? Common grace is incipient universalism, and universalism denies the cross.

The main concern of Psalm 73, however, is practical. Doubt of God's goodness to Israel and the related supposition that he is good to the ungodly are serious threats to the spiritual welfare of the child of God. So serious are the threats that "my feet were almost gone; my steps had well nigh slipped" (v. 2). Certain knowledge of God's goodness to Israel is necessary for salvation.

Am I a member by grace of God's Israel, the church? Do I have a clean heart? About this the believer has no doubt. Faith is assurance of living membership in the church. Then this also is true, and I ought to be convinced of it: God is good to me! Truly God is good to me!

CHAPTER TWO

The Wicked Seemingly Blessed

*But as for me, my feet were almost
gone; my steps had well nigh slipped.
For I was envious at the foolish, when I saw the
prosperity of the wicked* (Ps. 73:2, 3).

Almost Fallen

So important is the truth of God's goodness to Israel (that is, the clean of heart) that the spiritual welfare of the members of Israel depends upon it. It is not an overstatement to say that doubt of this truth jeopardizes the salvation of the clean of heart. The psalmist doubted the fundamental truth of the gospel laid down in verse 1. He supposed that the opposite was true. The truth that God is good to Israel is certain, but it is not always certain in the consciousness of the child of God: "But as for me" (v. 2).

The effect of this doubt upon the spiritual life of the doubting psalmist was that the doubt cast him into extreme spiritual peril. His feet almost gave way; his steps nearly slipped. Spiritual disaster threatened. If his feet give way and his steps slip, he is destroyed spiritually. He falls. Think of the feet of a mountain climber giving way on a steep slope, or of a soldier slipping and falling in battle. The reality would be that his faith in God gives way and is lost. The psalmist came near to doubting the goodness of God to him. This is unbelief. He was about to conclude that he washes his heart in vain (v. 13). Apostasy would follow, and the end of apostasy is spiritual and eternal destruction.

The experience of the psalmist is that of all the saints at some time in their lives. In the bitter trouble of our lives, we doubt the goodness of God to us. Doubting, we feel ourselves falling away from God, who is our salvation.

But the psalmist's feet did *not* go and his steps did *not* slip: "almost," but not quite; "well nigh," but not entirely. He is God's child, and God will not allow his child to fall away. God held his doubting child up in the end by the truth the psalmist had lost sight of: "Truly God is good to Israel."

The Great Temptation

The explanation of the doubt that cast the psalmist into mortal peril was the obvious prosperity of the wicked. The cause of his doubt of God's goodness to himself, the psalmist points out in verse 3, as is plain from the opening word, "for." The cause was "the prosperity of the wicked." As a rule, the wicked prosper. What the prosperity consists of, verses 4–12 describe in detail: earthly abundance and pleasures. Seemingly, everything goes well for the wicked in this life. Seemingly, this prosperity is God's blessing of the wicked. Seemingly, God favors them.

In contrast, the life of the psalmist was trouble-filled. He states this in verse 14: "All the day long have I been plagued, and chastened every morning." His own troubles are implied by his envying the wicked. They have what he lacks. The circumstances of his own life are the very opposite of their prosperous circumstances. Seemingly, the psalmist's troubles are God's curse upon his earthly life. Seemingly, God does not favor him.

The psalmist's envy was not merely resentment that people had more than he, or even that others had everything while he had nothing. Such a superficial understanding of the psalmist's envy, as though it were nothing more than the ignoble "green-eyed monster," would not do justice to the profound spiritual struggle of the God-fearing man. His envy was the deep-seated discontent that God seemed to bless the wicked, who hate him, whereas he seemed to withhold blessing from his own child, who loves and serves him.

The envy was wrong, grievously wrong, but only because it rested on a mistaken assumption. The assumption was that prosperity is grace and riches are blessing. Its corollary is that adversity is disfavor and poverty is curse. If the assumption of the psalmist was correct, he had every right to be envious of the wicked, just as a well-behaved child whose father deprives him of every good thing and even beats him daily, but shows every token of love to a depraved boy in the neighborhood and loads that rascally neighbor boy with good things, might well envy the neighbor boy. Who would blame the son for thinking, "I could better be the scoundrel who lives next door"?

Significantly, the word translated "prosperity" in verse 3 is the Hebrew word *shalom*. "I was envious...when I saw the *shalom* of the wicked." *Shalom* is the peace and plenty God promises to his covenant people in his covenant grace. The fear of the psalmist was that God gives *shalom* to the ungodly, those outside his spiritual family, and withholds *shalom* from his own children. This fear gave rise to envy, and envy toyed with the notion, "What is the use of fearing God? I might better live like the wicked."

The Only Safeguard

Against this grievous, dangerous temptation, to which no Christian is a stranger, there is one safeguard, and one safeguard only. The safeguard is the truth, "Truly good to Israel is God," with its implication, "and he is not good to the ungodly."

Sound, faithful preachers of the gospel must preach this truth. They must not proclaim to the wealthy, healthy, fat, old infidel, who stops cursing, drinking, and fornicating only long enough to say, "I sure am blessed," "Yes, indeed, God is gracious to you and blesses you abundantly." If preachers want to be free of the blood of such unbelievers, they must rather proclaim, "If you think you are blessed by God, you are a fool! The wrath of God is destroying you with every dollar you invest, every lobster you eat, and every breath you take! There is no blessing in unbelief and wickedness! None! There is no *shalom* for the ungodly, not in the eternity that is coming and not in this life! Repent!"

The faithful minister of the word must be especially sure that he preaches this aspect of the blessed gospel to Christ's suffering saints. To the parents weeping at the grave of a child (while the unbelieving neighbors enjoy healthy children), to the young mother dying of cancer (while her ungodly neighbor is full of life), to the husband whose wife has sinfully abandoned him (while his godless neighbor is happily married), to the laborer who has lost his job (while the wicked neighbor keeps his job), the pastor must not bring the message that the prosperity of the wicked is God's gracious blessing of them. To the saints in their suffering, this message necessarily carries the evil tidings that their own adversities are evidence of divine disfavor. But let the minister say this to the suffering people of God at the graveside, in the hospital, and at the deathbed: "God is good to Israel. Truly God is good to Israel."

CHAPTER THREE

The Troublesome Prosperity of the Wicked

For there are no bands in their death: but their strength is firm.
They are not in trouble as other men; neither are
they plagued like other men.
Therefore pride compasseth them about as a chain; violence
covereth them as a garment.
Their eyes stand out with fatness: they have more than heart could wish.
They are corrupt, and speak wickedly concerning oppression:
they speak loftily.
They set their mouth against the heavens, and their tongue
walketh through the earth.
Therefore his people return hither: and waters of a full cup are
wrung out to them.
And they say, How doth God know? and is there
knowledge in the most High?
Behold, these are the ungodly, who prosper in the world;
they increase in riches (Ps. 73:4–12).

THE psalmist went through a grievous spiritual struggle: his feet were almost gone, and his steps had well nigh slipped (v. 2). His faith in God faltered. Spiritual disaster threatened. The seriousness of this particular struggle in the experience of every child of God may not be minimized.

The believer at times yields to the temptation to envy the foolish. This envy involves doubting that God is good to Israel, particularly to oneself as a member of Israel.

One aspect of the occasion of this spiritual struggle is described in verses 4–12. The other aspect of the occasion of the struggle, closely related to that described in verses 4–12, is given in verse 14: "All the day long have I been plagued, and chastened every morning." When these two realities live in the soul of the child of God—what he sees of the prosperous earthly life of the wicked and his own experience of earthly troubles, contrasting sharply and painfully with the prosperity of the wicked—the occasion of a grievous spiritual struggle on the part of the God-fearing man or woman is present.

Fat Faces

Verses 4–12 are a full, detailed account of that aspect of the occasion of the psalmist's spiritual struggle that consists of the prosperity of the wicked. That such people prosper so is the reason, in part, why the child of God nearly falls in his faith.

Ease and prosperity characterize the earthly lives of the wicked. Their lives are free of the troubles that are common to the race, according to verse 5: serious illness; the ruin of their crops by drought, flooding, or insects; the bankruptcy of their business; the untimely death of a loved one.

Positively, they have an abundance of everything that makes earthly life comfortable and pleasurable. Not only do they have the necessities of life, lacking nothing, but they also have abundance. Verse 12 and the second part of verse 7 observe that they have riches and increase in them. Where the Authorized Version translates, "they have more than heart could wish," the Hebrew original expresses that whatever the heart imagines, like an overflowing river, they have. No luxury, no self-indulgent pleasure, is denied them. That they are rich is implied in the first part of verse 7, as well as that they enjoy good health—disgustingly good health. Their eyes bulge from their fat faces. Biblically, a fat face is not an evil, to be deplored and energetically to be gotten rid of by strenuous exercises, but a natural good. It shows that one is able to eat well and that he is healthy.

The prosperous wicked also know how to enjoy their trouble-free, rich lives. It is obvious that these people are not depressed in the midst of their plenty. This is evident from their reaction to their privileged life: "pride compasseth them about as a chain" (v. 6). In addition, according to the literal translation of verse 12, they are at ease in the world: "These are the ungodly, who are at ease in the world."

Further, this seemingly delightful state of affairs goes on for them without interruption as long as they live. The translators of the Authorized Version omitted the significant word "everlastingly" in verse 12: "These are the ungodly, who are *everlastingly* at ease in the world." Their trouble-free, healthy, comfortable lives continue right up to the moment of their death. With this, the psalmist begins his spiritual struggle. Verse 4 begins, "For there are no bands in their death." Some who explain the psalm, including Franz Delitzsch, find it inappropriate that the psalmist would begin the account of the prosperity of the wicked with a reference to their death. It does not seem right to them that the psalmist would describe the dying of the wicked before he said anything about their living. Delitzsch, therefore, performs some fascinating legerdemain upon the Hebrew text of verse 4, so that it will read: "For they suffer no pangs, healthy and fat is their belly."[1] The mention of death is removed.

But the psalmist starts with the death of the wicked for good reason. The easy death of the wicked is especially troublesome to him. There, finally, it should be evident that the wicked are cursed and punished. There, at last, the wicked should be stricken, like Herod, with horrible, painful disease and should cry out in misery. But even there, at his earthly end, it is not so. Rather, the wicked come to a peaceful end, dying of a sudden heart attack at a ripe, old age, or fading away painlessly in their sleep.

They are physically healthy right to the end, as the literal translation of the second part of verse 4 brings out: "fat is their belly." Their peaceful, unconcerned mental state is also in view: "no bands in their death." They die without pangs of conscience. They have no regrets. Seemingly, they die without a care in the world. They show no struggle over their sins, no conflict with the devil, no fear of impending judgment. As a fat

---

1. Franz Delitzsch, *Biblical Commentary on the Psalms*, trans. Francis Bolton, vol. 2 of *Biblical Commentary on the Old Testament* (Grand Rapids, MI: Eerdmans, 1959), 308.

steer waddles contentedly into the slaughterhouse, so the wicked take leave of this life.

How different, often, is the death of the God-fearing man! His body is racked with excruciating pain. He dies inch by painful inch over months and years. At the very end, on his deathbed, he struggles over the guilt of his sinfulness and sins, contends with gloomy doubts of his salvation, and fights with Satan.

"Behold," exclaims the psalmist in verse 12, summing up, "these are the ungodly, who are everlastingly at ease...they increase in riches." Prosperity is not the condition of all wicked men without exception, of course. The psalmist knew as well as we do of exceptions. He knew of wicked men and women who come to grief in one way or another. Elsewhere the psalms themselves teach that some wicked persons suffer various miseries and come to untimely, wretched ends. Nevertheless, prosperity is the condition of many wicked men and women. What is intended in Psalm 73 is that the wicked generally prosper, whereas the godly are always plagued and chastened.

Divine Fattening

The prosperous earthly condition of the life of the wicked does not happen accidentally. Nor is their prosperity due to their greater industriousness or to their superior shrewdness. Rather, their prosperity is God's doing. The psalmist knows this. God gives them prosperity. It is God who arranges the circumstances of their lives so that they live at ease and die in tranquillity, just as it is God who plagues and chastens the psalmist. Exactly this is the psalmist's problem. For his temptation is to suppose that the prosperity of the wicked is God's blessing of them in his grace, whereas his plaguing of the psalmist is his failure to bless.

That God bestows the prosperity of the wicked is stated in verse 18. With reference to this prosperity, the inspired Scripture says, "*Thou* didst set them in slippery places." Ignoring for the present that the text explains God's act of prospering the wicked radically differently from those who view it as a blessing in (common) grace, we learn from verse 18, if we had any doubt about it, that the prosperous life of the wicked, right up to and including their easy death, is the deed of God: "Thou didst set," that is, "Thou didst give them a death without bands, their fat bellies, their trouble-free lives, their everlasting ease, and their abundant riches."

But these people are wicked and ungodly, whereas the plagued psalmist and all who are clean of heart are God's chosen Israel.

What shall we say of this prosperity of the wicked? Shall we say that it is a blessing, a manifestation of the grace of God toward them? If we say this, then we say the opposite of Psalm 73: "Thou didst set them in slippery places: thou castedst them down into destruction" (v. 18). If we say this, we say that God is gracious to the unrighteous and—by inescapable implication—that he is wrathful to those who, by faith in Christ, cleanse their heart and wash their hands. If we say that the prosperity of the wicked is divine blessing, then we give the faltering Christian, whose serious spiritual struggle is recorded in Psalm 73, the final push, so that his feet *do* fall and his steps *do* slip.

We will not say this of the prosperity of the wicked.

Rather, as the very first principle of the Christian religion, we will say, and believe, this: "Truly good to Israel is God."

Necessarily, at the same time we say this: "Truly God is not good to the wicked, even though they prosper in the world." "Truly in the very prospering of the wicked, God is not good to them." We should never think otherwise. Neither should they.

CHAPTER FOUR

The Wicked Who Prosper

For there are no bands in their death: but their strength is firm.
They are not in trouble as other men; neither are
they plagued like other men.
Therefore pride compasseth them about as a chain; violence
covereth them as a garment.
Their eyes stand out with fatness: they have more than heart could wish.
They are corrupt, and speak wickedly concerning oppression:
they speak loftily.
They set their mouth against the heavens, and their tongue
walketh through the earth.
Therefore his people return hither: and waters of a full cup are
wrung out to them.
And they say, How doth God know? and is there
knowledge in the most High?
Behold, these are the ungodly, who prosper in the world;
they increase in riches (Ps. 73:4–12).

THE psalmist tells us that he experienced a serious spiritual crisis. The feet of his faith in God were almost gone; his spiritual steps had well nigh slipped. "What," we ask, "was the occasion of this spiritual struggle?" Our question is urgent because we recognize that in Psalm 73 the Holy Spirit has inspired a full account of the struggle of everyone in every age who is member of Israel, that is, everyone who by faith in Jesus Christ has a clean heart. The struggle of the psalmist was to believe that God is good to Israel. More particularly, his struggle was to believe that God is good to Israel *in his providential government of Israel's everyday, earthly life in the world.* In this struggle, the psalmist was overcome—not completely, and certainly not finally—but partly and temporarily. He sinned. His sin was that he envied the foolish (v. 3).

There were two distinct aspects to the occasion of the struggle. One aspect was the "prosperity of the wicked" (v. 3). This prosperity is described in detail in verses 4–12. Summing up this aspect of the occasion of his struggle, the psalmist cries out in verse 12, "These are the ungodly, who are everlastingly at ease in the world; they increase in riches."

It is evident both in verse 3 and in verse 12 that another element enters powerfully into this first aspect of the occasion of the psalmist's struggle. His deep spiritual problem was not simply that certain men and women prosper. But his problem was also that those who prosper are "wicked" (v. 3) and "ungodly" (v. 12).

Proud

Those who prosper materially are proud, bold, defiant enemies of God and of his people. Psalm 73 emphasizes their pride. Verse 6 takes note of their pride and declares that these prosperous people are self-consciously and deliberately proud. They flaunt their pride, displaying it as one might ostentatiously wear a necklace for all to see. The "chain" in the Authorized Version's translation of verse 6 is one such necklace: "Pride compasseth them about as a chain." The Hebrew original reads, "Pride adorns them like a necklace." Pride is not truly beautiful, of course. But these people think so. They are openly and proudly proud. Pride is also the charge against them in verse 3, where the Authorized Version describes them as "foolish." The precise sense of this foolishness is their being arrogant boasters.

Proud to begin with in that they do not reverence God in their hearts, these fools allow themselves to be carried away by their prosperity—wealth, property, possessions, achievements, lifestyle, fame, and power—to heights of overweening arrogance. They are full of themselves because of their earthly success. They express their pride in bearing and in words. Like little Nebuchadnezzars, they strut about their farms, or businesses, or workplaces, or homes, or clubhouses, or senate office buildings, crowing, "Is not this great Babylon, that I have built for the house of the kingdom by the might of my power, and for the honour of my majesty?" (Dan. 4:30).

In their appalling exultation of themselves, they defy God. They deny God. If he exists, he does not matter as far as the earthly lives of these men and women are concerned. What Pierre Laplace haughtily said to Napoleon concerning any dependency of science and scientists upon God, these people say concerning any dependency of human life upon God whatsoever: "I had no need of that hypothesis."[1] This is to bring pride to its highest pitch. According to verse 8, "they speak loftily." They speak thus from the heights of their self-exultation against God: "They set their mouth against the heavens," as the dwelling place of God (v. 9).

This is what they say against the one who dwells in the heavens: "How doth God know? and is there knowledge in the most High?" (v. 11). Here there is a certain acknowledgment of God. Despite themselves, these heaven-defying boasters betray a certain knowledge of the true God, as their use of his name, "most High," shows. Even proud, apostate fools, drunk with earthly success and mad in the worship of Mammon, cannot entirely escape knowing that God is, for God invincibly reveals the truth of himself to them (Rom. 1:18–32). But they deny that he knows. That is, they deny that his knowledge (if indeed he is a knowing God) has anything to do with human life in the world, its success or its failure, its happiness or its misery, its worth or its emptiness. If his knowledge has nothing to do with human life, then neither does his will affect human life. God himself, therefore, is not a factor in human life. No one needs to reckon with God with regard to earthly life. Autonomous man governs his life by his knowledge and will.

In this way, the prosperous proud deny the God whom they know. For if there is no knowledge in the most high—*sovereign*

---

1. Quoted in E. T. Bell, *Men of Mathematics: The Lives and Achievements of the Great Mathematicians from Zeno to Poincaré* (New York: Simon and Schuster, 1937), 181.

knowledge of the earthly life of every human, knowledge that is the main fac-
tor in the life of every human, knowledge upon which the earthly life of every
man and woman depends, knowledge that determines the success or failure,
happiness or misery, worth or emptiness of the life of every human, indeed,
knowledge that accounts for the existence and circumstances of every hu-
man—God is not the "most High."

But the proud have an argument for their contention that
there is no knowledge in the most high. There is a reason for
their daring question, "How doth God know?" The reason the
proud deny God's knowledge is the same as the reason for
the struggle of the psalmist: the prosperity of the wicked and
the plaguing of the clean of heart. Seemingly, God does not
bless the godly as a reward of their godliness, nor does he curse
the wicked in punishment of their ungodliness. Rather, seemingly, he curses the righteous and blesses the unrighteous. Vice
is ascendant, and virtue goes under. The God-fearing cleanse
their hearts in vain. The ungodly have nothing to fear from the
God revealed in Holy Scripture and preached by the church.
"Let us speak loftily! Let us blaspheme!" they cry.

Not only do the proud blaspheme God in the heavens.
They also oppress God's people. Their chief weapon is the
tongue. It "walketh through the earth" (v. 9). A literal reading
of verse 8 brings out clearly this manifestation of their pride:
"They deride and speak wickedly; they speak oppression from
the heights." They *speak* oppression. They oppress the saints by
their cruel speech. They jeer at the humble, who fear God and
acknowledge him in all their ways. Especially when the proud
see the godly plagued and chastened, they deride them and

their ridiculous piety. The proud have always spoken oppression in their conversation. Today they speak oppression in their books and magazines, in their television programs and movies, in their humanistic, naturalistic, and evolutionistic education, and in their apostate religion. This is part of the plaguing of the child of God mentioned in verse 14.

We must not suppose that these proud boasters are only a few, exceptionally daring men, a Friedrich Nietzsche, a Bertrand Russell, a William Ernest Henley, and other avowed atheists. Pride is simply that one does not know himself a sinful creature, completely dependent upon God for everything, one's next breath as well as the forgiveness of sins. Arrogant defiance of God is simply that this self-confident person does not need God, can provide for himself, and will take care of his own life. "I am the master of my fate: / I am the captain of my soul."[2] The proud of Psalm 73 are simply independent, sovereign men and women. The "Christian" West is full of these people. Nominally Christian churches are full of these people. Such proud people may also be found in true churches of Christ. They were found in Old Testament Israel.

Unrighteous

The fundamental spiritual state of those who prosper is unrighteousness. Twice in verses 3–12, the psalmist describes

---

2. William Ernest Henley, "Invictus" in *Immortal Poems of the English Language,* ed. Oscar Williams (New York: Simon and Schuster, 1952), 475, 476.

them as unrighteous. The word translated "wicked" in verse 3 is the same word translated "ungodly" in verse 12. The basic meaning of the Hebrew word is "unrighteous." This is evident in Genesis 18:23, where the word (translated "wicked") is contrasted with the word that means "righteous": "Wilt thou also destroy the righteous with the wicked?" Those who prosper are wicked and ungodly in the sense of being unrighteous. As unrighteous, their legal position, their standing, before God the judge is that of radical disharmony with his law and with the righteousness of his own good being. God is good to Israel. He is also good in himself. One of the perfections that makes him good is righteousness. His righteousness is revealed in his law. With this law and with the righteousness reflected in the law, the prosperous wicked are at odds. Their deeds, their words, and their entire lives are opposed to God. They do not love and obey his law, which they know. Their deeds, words, and entire lives express a rebel-nature. Above all, they do not believe in God, through the coming Messiah, for imputed righteousness.

As unrighteous, the proud blasphemers of God and oppressors of God's people are guilty. They are worthy of the divine curse. They are worthy only of divine curse. As God is righteous, they *must* be cursed both in time and in eternity. But, seemingly, they are blessed. The unrighteous prosper, and it is God who prospers them. In contrast, the psalmist, who believes in God and is, by this believing, righteous, seemingly is cursed with plaguing and chastening.

Just as reflection on who prospers in the world should have kept the psalmist from supposing that these men and women are blessed, so should this reflection keep Christians today from supposing that prosperity is blessing for the wicked. If only we remember who these persons are, we will not envy them. The Bible teaches that God detests the proud and curses them. "Thou hast rebuked the proud that are cursed, which do err from thy commandments" (Ps. 119:21). The Bible is clear that, apart from the basis of righteousness, there is no blessing of sinful humans. In Galatians 3, the apostle teaches that the blessing of the nations depends squarely upon justification by faith on the basis of the redeeming cross of Christ. "And the scripture, foreseeing that God would justify the heathen through faith, preached before the gospel unto Abraham, saying, In thee shall all nations be blessed. So then they which be of faith are blessed with faithful Abraham" (Gal. 3:8, 9). Apart from the righteousness of faith on the basis of the death of Christ, there is only the curse of God upon sinners. "Cursed is every one that continueth not in all things which are written in the book of the law to do them" (Gal. 3:10). God does not bless the unrighteous. God curses the unrighteous. Galatians 3:10 is a quotation of Deuteronomy 27:26. Already in the Old Testament Scriptures, God made known that he does not bless the unrighteous. The psalmist should have known better than to suppose that the prosperity of the unrighteous was God's blessing of them.

Regardless how the prosperous, trouble-free lives of proud, unrighteous men and women appear to us, ready as we are to assume that riches are blessing, God has no favor toward the unrighteous. He does not bless them.

To envy these proud, unrighteous people is foolish, even beastly, as the psalmist comes to know, according to verse 22.

Increasingly Evil

One striking aspect of the wickedness of those who prosper in the world is that it increases on account of the prosperity. This may not be overlooked. It is important for dispelling the psalmist's (and our) fear that the prosperity of the wicked is God's blessing of them in his goodness toward them. Prosperity makes them more and more wicked. Corrupt by conception and birth, they become increasingly evil by means of their earthly prosperity. Their wickedness intensifies.

Verse 6 teaches that the cause of their pride is their ease and prosperity. Verse 5 observes that "they are not in trouble as other men; neither are they plagued like other men." *"Therefore,"* declares verse 6, "pride compasseth them about as a chain." Because of their trouble-free life, they add pride to their wickedness. Prosperity emboldens them blasphemously to challenge the most High: "How doth God know?" (v. 11).

Not only does prosperity intensify the wickedness of the ungodly who enjoy this prosperity, but it also spreads wickedness in the human race. This is the thought of verse 10: "Therefore his people return hither: and waters of a full cup are wrung out to them." Rightly understood, verse 10 teaches that the prosperity of the ungodly man influences many, even within the covenant community, to throw in their lot with this enemy of God.

The reference in the first part of verse 10 is not to God's people. "His" does not refer to God. Neither does the second part of verse 10 refer to the sufferings of God's people, as some suppose. The verse that immediately follows makes plain that the subject in verse 10 continues to be reprobate, ungodly people. Only they say, "How doth God know?" (v. 11). The suffering of God's people does not come up in the psalm until verse 13.

"His people" in verse 10 are the people of the prosperous, wicked man, who is described in verses 3–9. These many men are regarded in verse 10 as an individual. His earthly success and proud, confident boasting have the effect that many turn to him and his materialistic way of life. They drain, or suck out, the waters of the full cup of the prosperous boaster. This is figurative for their eager adoption of his earthly-mindedness and their enthusiastic involvement in his life of eating, drinking, buying, selling, marrying and giving in marriage, making merry, and blaspheming God. The cause is the prosperity of the wicked: "*Therefore* his people return hither" (v. 10). The prosperity of the ungodly ruins many.

A Strange "Grace"

What a strange effect, or fruit, of material prosperity, if these earthly riches and comfortable circumstances of wicked men and women are grace to these unrighteous scoffers at God and oppressors of God's people! This is the teaching of many: The prosperity of the wicked is the common grace of God to them. Here then is a grace of God that does not make a man a whit better, does not deliver him from sin, does not make him good. Rather, here is a grace of God that *increases* wickedness! Here is a grace of God that multiplies open, proud, defiant enemies of God!

This is what prosperity—rain and sunshine in season, riches, health, every material possession the carnal heart could desire, a comfortable life right up to the moment of death—does to the wicked, according to Psalm 73. It increases wickedness. "*Therefore,*" that is, because they are not in trouble, because they prosper materially, pride adorns them like a necklace (v. 6). "*Therefore,*" that is, because the ungodly prosper in their arrogance against, and independency from, God, many people turn to the proud boaster and drink deeply from his full cup (v. 10).

The authoritative spokesman for the theory of a common grace of God, Abraham Kuyper, acknowledged that the final fruit of common grace in history will be the godless, depraved, persecuting culture of Antichrist.[3] This is the unavoidable conclusion, if one views the prosperity and natural abilities of the wicked as grace. Grace—the grace *of God*—produces the beast and the beastly kingdom!

Some grace! If the material prosperity of the wicked is indeed grace, well may we earnestly pray, "God, spare me your common grace. All it does is intensify wickedness in the one who receives it and spread wickedness throughout the human race."

---

3. Abraham Kuyper, "Common Grace," in *Abraham Kuyper: A Centennial Reader,* ed. James D. Bratt (Grand Rapids, MI: Eerdmans, 1998), 179–182.

But at one point in his pilgrimage, the psalmist thought that the prosperity of the wicked is grace. It lived in his soul, "The ungodly prosper, and this prosperity is due to divine blessing." Necessarily accompanying this notion was the discouraging supposition, "My own earthly troubles are God's wrathful curse, or, at least, a distinct lack of blessing."

The psalmist stumbled, and we stumble likewise over the same problem: the prosperity of the enemies of God; the seeming blessing of lives lived in disregard for, and opposition to, God.

We forget, as the psalmist forgot, a fundamental truth of the gospel: "Truly God is good to Israel." We forget as well the implied truth, which is equally fundamental: "Truly God is *not* good to the unrighteous."

CHAPTER FIVE

The Godly Seemingly Cursed

Verily I have cleansed my heart in vain,
and washed my hands in innocency.
For all the day long have I been plagued,
and chastened every morning.
If I say, I will speak thus; behold, I should offend
against the generation of thy children.
When I thought to know this, it was too painful
for me (Ps. 73:13–16).

THE psalmist was severely shaken regarding his faith in God: "My feet were almost gone; my steps had well nigh slipped" (v. 2). The occasion of this crisis was twofold. One aspect was the prosperity of the wicked. This is the subject of verses 3–12. The other aspect of the struggle of the psalmist, and of every godly man and woman in every age, is identified in verses 13–16.

The relationship of these four verses is as follows. That which caused the psalmist to stumble and almost fall is briefly set forth in verse 14: "All the day long have I been plagued, and chastened every morning." Verse 16 not only describes the mental anguish that the fact of verse 14 caused the psalmist, but also declares the whole matter of the prosperity of the wicked and the suffering of the saints to be an insoluble problem to the mind of man. "When I thought to know this, it was too painful for me" (v. 16). In the second part of verse 16, the Hebrew original has, "It was wearisome labor to me." But the matter was also a problem he could not figure out. The problem is solved only in the sanctuary, where the word of God sheds light on the end both of the ungodly and of the godly.

In verse 13, the psalmist informs us of the conclusion he came to from seeing the prosperity of the unrighteous and experiencing his own troubles. "Verily," he decided, "I have cleansed my heart in vain, and washed my hands in innocency." This was the almost going of his feet and the well nigh slipping of his steps confessed in verse 2. At this precise point, when he said this to himself, his faith faltered, and spiritual ruin threatened.

But verse 15 is evidence that, although he stumbled, the psalmist did not fall. In his worst moment, when he despaired of God and his goodness, God was holding him up, although the psalmist did not realize this until later. There was a ray of light in the darkness of the psalmist's doubt of the goodness of God and despair of the worth of serving God. The psalmist continued to have a concern for God's people. "I have cleansed my heart in vain" was what he said to himself. Deliberately, he refrained from saying this to others, lest "I should offend against the generation of thy children" (v. 15). He loved the children of God. He did not want to cause any of them to stumble and fall, as they might if he would announce that it is useless to serve God. In the midst of his folly and unbelief, he continued to wash his heart.

Earthly Troubles

The second aspect of the occasion of the psalmist's spiritual struggle was his own painful troubles. Of the ungodly he says in verse 5, "They are not in trouble," while in verse 14 he complains that the godly man or woman has troubles, all kinds of troubles.

The brevity of the account of the troubles of the godly in comparison with the lengthy description of the prosperity of the wicked must not lead us to minimize the severity of the troubles of the godly man or woman. They are "plagues," that is, destructive evils inflicting untold misery. With regard to the devastation of earthly life and the resulting misery, we think of the plagues by which God destroyed Egypt. The troubles of the righteous are a "chastening," that is, a beating or whipping.

The severity of the troubles is indicated by their duration and repetition: "all the day long" and "every morning" (v. 14). The meaning is not that there is nothing but troubles in the life of the believers. This would not be realistic; there are also pleasures and times of gladness. But the meaning is that there are always troubles. There is no let-up, no relief. One trouble follows another. There are troubles in youth, troubles in middle age, and troubles in old age. Some of the troubles are so intense that the pain of them is with the child of God constantly. Even though the event that caused the misery is in the past, the

painful consequences and disturbing memory of the evil endure. Every morning anew the child of God awakes to the
prospect of some new trouble or with the lingering effects of
an old one. These troubles temper his or her enjoyment of the
pleasures of life.

The troubles of the righteous in Psalm 73 are not spiritual
difficulties. They are the occasion of spiritual difficulties, but
they are not themselves spiritual difficulties. They are earthly
evils of various kinds. The subject of Psalm 73 is the earthly circumstances of human life. Just as the prosperity of the wicked
is physical health, financial wealth, success in farming or business, and earthly ease, so the plaguing and chastening of the
righteous are sickness; financial distress and poverty; setbacks
and even failures in business, farming, or labor; family prob-
lems; and earthly unease. Whereas the sun shines and the rain
falls on the fields of the ungodly at just the right time and in
just the right amount to make the ungodly farmer a prosperous
man, the same sun burns, or the same rain floods, the fields of
the godly farmer to bankrupt him. Probably, he must hire himself out to his prosperous neighbor in order to eke out a living.

God's Plaguing

These troubles come from God, as the righteous man knows
very well. The Israelite knew who plagued and chastened him,
just as he knew who caused the prosperity of the wicked. Not
for one minute did a God-fearing Israelite, as the psalmist
surely was, doubt the sovereignty of God over the evils in his

life. This was not his problem. His problem was exactly that God destroyed his earthly life and whipped him all day long, and the psalmist knew it.

Those Reformed philosophers in the twenty-first century a.d., who attempt to solve the problem of evils in human life by denying God's sovereign government of evils, not only fail to solve the problem of evils but also create the additional, enormous problem of a god who is not God. If God is not sovereign over evils, he is not God. A god who is powerless over evils is not the God made known in the Bible, particularly in the psalms. Concerning the heavy stroke—an extraordinary evil—for example, that reduced the psalmist to silence in Psalm 39, the psalmist confesses, "Thou didst it" (v. 9). Denial of God's sovereignty over the evils in human life certainly rules out the possibility of ever viewing these evils as divine blessings with a good outcome, which is the comfort finally afforded the psalmist in Psalm 73.

God sent the troubles which plagued and chastened the psalmist, but the troubles were not direct judgments upon specific presumptuous sins for which the psalmist did not repent. If this were the case, the psalmist would not have had a problem with the troubles. He knew, as do all Christians, that deliberate, great sins require severe judgments. If we deliberately commit sin and stubbornly walk in it, the ensuing troubles are not a problem for us. We know very well why God sends the evils.

The psalmist was a man who was always cleansing his heart and washing his hands in innocency (v. 13). This is the activity of sanctification in both its inward and outward aspects. Inwardly, in his heart, he consecrated himself to God in thankful love toward God as the God of his salvation. Outwardly, with his hands, he served God by deeds of love for God and for his neighbor. The psalmist was one of those who had a "clean heart" by the regenerating Spirit of holiness (v. 1). Still the plagues came! Despite his godliness, the heavy blows fell!

These troubles were his lot in contrast to the prospering of the wicked. By virtue of their severity and duration, the troubles were hard enough to bear by themselves. Knowledge that all the while the ungodly had no troubles but were everlastingly at ease made the psalmist's experience all but unbearable.

It seemed as if God prospered his enemies and plagued his covenant friends. The righteous he beat, whereas the unrighteous were untouched.

Giving up on God

This reality of earthly life and its circumstances becomes the occasion of a powerful, dangerous temptation to the godly man or woman. So powerful a temptation is this, that it does what all the other temptations in the life of the godly—the temptation of pride, the temptation of setting one's heart on riches, the temptation of sexual lust—cannot accomplish. The child of God is strongly inclined to cease cleansing his heart and washing his hands, that is, to give up the Christian life of holiness and discipleship. Overcome by this temptation, he becomes bitter and despondent. So dangerous a temptation is this, that he is almost spiritually destroyed: "My feet were almost gone; my steps had well nigh slipped" (v. 2).

The prosperity of the ungodly and his own contrasting troubles with regard to the circumstances of earthly life are the occasion for the believer's giving up on God: "Verily I have cleansed my heart in vain, and washed my hands in innocency" (v. 13). "In vain" modifies both parts of verse 13: In vain I have cleansed my heart, and in vain I have washed my hands so that my deeds were innocent. The whole of the Christian life of serving God is for nothing, since the Christian gets only troubles for his reward, while the ungodly man, whose heart and hands are filthy with wickedness, prospers.

This reaction of the psalmist to his own troubles and to the prosperity of the wicked was foolish and ignorant, *sinfully* foolish and ignorant, as he freely confesses in verse 22: "So foolish was I, and ignorant." Is this why the God-fearing person lives a holy life? To prosper in this life with earthly riches and ease? Is this brief earthly life so important to him? Are perishing earthly goods of such ultimate worth to him?

And is not the explanation of the troubles of the godly, as well as the explanation of the lack of troubles of the ungodly, obvious? Is not the explanation indicated in one of the very words with which the psalmist describes his troubles, the word "chastening"? God chastens his children, whom he loves. Addressing the same temptation that stumbled the psalmist, the author of the epistle to the Hebrews reminds the children of God: "For whom the Lord loveth he chasteneth, and scourgeth every son whom he receiveth" (Heb. 12:6). The psalmist solves the problem of the troubles of the citizens of Israel, including himself (although he does not realize it), by the name he calls these people: "thy children." Of course, they will have troubles in this life. God is their Father.

As a good Father, God chastens his children so that they will cleanse their hearts and wash their hands in innocency all the more. They must sanctify themselves by disciplining, indeed, crucifying, their sinful nature. They must sanctify themselves by taking their affections off this earthly life and its treasures and setting their affections on the coming heavenly life with its treasures. They must sanctify themselves by confessing God's goodness in their troubles, indeed, in circumstances of the utter destruction of their earthly life, so that they may prove to the enemy and to themselves that their service of God is selfless—not for the sake of their own earthly prosperity, but for the sake of his glory.

As for the trouble-free lives of the reprobate ungodly, should this be such a problem to the psalmist, and to us? God cares nothing for them. They are not his children. The true Israel, those who are clean of heart, are "the generation of thy children" (Ps. 73:15), not the wicked who are only outwardly members of the nation, or the wicked outside the nation. God is not their Father. He lets them go in their unholy, wicked way, undisciplined, without the chastening children must have. Hebrews 12 continues: "But if ye be without chastisement, whereof all are partakers, then are ye bastards, and not sons" (v. 8). Indeed, as the psalmist comes to understand, God hardens them in their godlessness by the very prosperity he gives them.

Nevertheless, such was the weakness of the psalmist that the prosperity of the wicked in contrast to his own troubles was the occasion of a powerful temptation. Such is also our experience. There is the time of a certain grievous disappointment, of a shattering loss, of a devastating evil. In bitterness of soul, we cry out (to ourselves), "I have served God for nothing! My holy life in the church has been wasted! I quit!"

"*Verily,*" we convince ourselves, it is senseless to serve God.

Make no mistake, the issue, whether God blesses the ungodly with a (common) grace, is no academic, abstractly theological matter, nor is it a minor matter. Doubtful about this issue, the psalmist found himself doubting a fundamental truth of the gospel of salvation: "Truly God is good to Israel." Doubting this truth, he stumbled and almost fell.

CHAPTER SIX

Help in the Sanctuary

Until I went into the sanctuary of God; then
understood I their end (Ps. 73:17).

The All-Important "End"

WHAT saved the psalmist, what kept his feet from going completely and his steps from slipping, was his understanding of the end of the prosperous wicked.

The connection between verse 16 and verse 17 is this: Attempting to figure out the meaning of the prosperity of the wicked and the troubles of the saints, particularly his own troubles, the psalmist was baffled. Not only was he unable to make sense of the hard facts of his experience, but wrestling with them in his mind left him anguished. Trying to make sense of the prosperity of the wicked in contrast to his own troubled life was, according to the literal translation of verse 16, "wearisome labor to me." What especially baffled and distressed him was the seeming contradiction of the truth that God is good to Israel by these hard facts of everyday life. The psalmist was baffled and distressed *until he understood the end of the wicked.* He understood their end only in the sanctuary of God.

The end of the prosperous wicked, in distinction from their present earthly life as the way to their end, is their death. Their end is their physical death as the entrance into an everlasting existence. Death ushers them into eternity. What their end consists of, verses 18–20 describe. In one word, it is "destruction" (v. 18). Physical death is not for them the mere extinction of earthly life, as they like to think, so that many of them are able peacefully to face the prospect of death. "There are no bands in their death" (v. 4). Rather, death is their falling into the hands of an angry God, so that their physical death is the beginning of eternal death.

This is the end of the wicked, not in the sense merely that death cuts off their prosperous earthly life. This is indeed the case, and this is bad enough for those who have no other treasures than the material riches they lose at death. But death is their end also in the sense that their prosperous earthly life naturally and inevitably moves toward this end. Their prosperous life issues in this end. It has this end as its certain, rightful goal. Death as its end is inherent in the prosperous life of the wicked, as a violent storm is the inherent end in the towering thundercloud on a hot, humid afternoon in the mid-west United States. To this end, their prosperity is always bringing them. In this end, their prosperity has its meaning. Unto this end, their prosperity is the means.

It is foolish, it is utterly mistaken, it is forbidden, it is impossible, to evaluate the earthly prosperity of the wicked apart from the end of this prosperity and their prosperous lives. In order rightly to judge their prosperity, we must ask, "Where does this prosperity bring them? Where does God intend that it bring them?"

The same is true of the troubles in our own lives. Look at these troubles apart from our end, and we God-fearing people will conclude that God does not bless us. Indeed, he curses us. But our trouble-filled lives also have an end. Verse 24 refers to our end: "afterward." This end is "glory" (v. 24). We must view our present lives of chastening and plaguing, not apart from their end, but in light of it.

In light of the end of the prosperous wicked, all the prosperity of the wicked is seen to be curse, only curse. In light of the end of the troubled saints, all their troubles are blessing, only blessing.

"Truly God is good to Israel."

"Truly God is good to Israel"—*in everyday, earthly life.*

Truly good is God to *Israel,* and *only* to Israel, in everyday, earthly life.

Truly God is not good to the wicked in his burying them in prosperity.

Doing a Theology of Things at Church

This, we believers come, finally, to understand, and we understand the truth about the prosperity of the wicked in God's sanctuary: "until I went into the sanctuary of God." With regard to determining God's blessing and cursing, we may not depend on what we observe with our physical senses. We may not make our evaluation on the basis of our feelings. We cannot arrive at the truth even by our reason, if we use our minds outside the sanctuary. Verse 16 teaches that when the psalmist "thought to know" the truth of the great matter of the prosperity of the wicked in contrast to the troubles of the righteous, he came to a dead end, and was pained besides.

Theologians may not do theology concerning the meaning of rain and sunshine on the fields of ungodly farmers or of the impressive culture of godless societies on the corner of Monroe and Division in downtown Grand Rapids, Michigan, or on the streets of southern California. If they do, they will invariably and necessarily go wrong, to the discomfort of the suffering people of God and to the illicit and misleading comfort of the wicked.

The psalmist did his inspired theology concerning rain and sunshine, riches, health, family, and ease in the sanctuary of God. That was the holy place where Jehovah God dwelled with his covenant people above the ark on the throne of the mercy seat. In Asaph's day, the sanctuary was a tent in Jerusalem. Today, the sanctuary of God is the assembly of believers and their children on the Lord's day. The triune God is present in this assembly in the preaching of the gospel of the cross of Jesus Christ and in the sacraments. There, and only there, we understand the end of the prosperous wicked. There we are delivered from the dreadful doubt, whether God blesses the wicked and curses the righteous in the circumstances of earthly life. There our feet are kept from going, and our steps from slipping, supposing that God is gracious to the ungodly and ungracious to us.

Why in the sanctuary?

In the sanctuary is the word of God that reveals the truth about time and eternity, about this life and the life to come, and about the relation between temporal life and the coming eternity. In the sanctuary God makes known the unseen things of eternal life and eternal death. In the sanctuary is the gospel of everlasting, all-embracing grace to all who fear God, cleansing their hearts and washing their hands, as well as the warning of wrath upon all who hate him. In the sanctuary is the message and sign of the cross of Jesus Christ, which has lifted all curse from elect Israel in time and to all eternity. In the sanctuary the same message of the cross testifies that the curse abides on all who are outside of Christ in unbelief—in time and to all eternity.

In the sanctuary the gospel and Spirit of Jesus Christ convince the struggling children of God, as they convinced the doubting psalmist, "Truly God is good to Israel."

CHAPTER SEVEN

The End of the Prosperous Wicked

Surely thou didst set them in slippery places: thou castedst
them down into destruction.
How are they brought into desolation, as in a moment! they are
utterly consumed with terrors (Ps. 73:18, 19).

IN the sanctuary of God, where God makes known the truth about the prosperous life of the wicked and the troublous life of his Israel, the God-fearing man or woman is delivered from his or her great temptation, occasioned by these two contrasting lives. God delivers the struggling saint by revealing the "end" of the prosperous wicked (v. 17).

What the end of the wicked is, we learn in verses 18 and 19. These verses warn of the end of all the wicked—the wicked within the visible church and the wicked in the openly unbelieving world of the ungodly.

By the "end" of the wicked, verse 17 has in view their final destiny and eternal state. They reach this end when their earthly life ends in physical death. At the instant of physical death begins their end. This life is not all there is for the wicked, any more than it is for the righteous. There is also an end for them. This end is everlasting.

Destruction

The end of the wicked is their utter destruction. Verses 18 and 19, describing the end of the wicked, use four powerful words, all of which have the idea of the wasting and ruining of the wicked. There are the words correctly translated by the Authorized Version as "destruction" and "desolation." In verse 19, where the Authorized Version reads, "they are utterly consumed," the Hebrew original has two expressive verbs in succession: "they perish, they are consumed." Leupold suggests the translation, "they are done for, they are consumed."[1] Their end is terrible.

The prosperous earthly life of the wicked man or woman is destroyed, as is the arrogance with which he or she exalted himself or herself against God and his children. Still more, and far worse, the wicked person is constantly, everlastingly destroyed, desolated, caused to perish, and consumed.

This is one of the passages in the Old Testament that makes known the destiny of the wicked after death. Old Testament Scripture does not sharply distinguish the state of the wicked in their soul before the resurrection of the body and the state of the wicked in soul and body after the resurrection of the

1. H. C. Leupold, *Exposition of the Psalms* (Grand Rapids, MI: Baker, 1974), 527.

body, as the New Testament does. In keeping with the less developed doctrine of the Old Testament, this passage simply speaks of the destruction of the wicked as an undifferentiated reality. Since this destruction begins at the instant of physical death and since the bodies of the wicked rot in the grave until the resurrection in the day of Christ, the passage teaches a destruction of the wicked in their soul immediately upon their dying. In light of the teaching of Scripture elsewhere, including Daniel 12:2, that the bodies of the wicked will be raised "to shame and everlasting contempt," the destruction of the wicked will culminate in their being consumed in both soul and body.

The Terrors of God

The one who inflicts the destruction upon the wicked is God. This is the express teaching of verse 18: "Thou [God] castedst them down into destruction." The wicked are desolated, caused to perish, and consumed by God. That God is the destroyer of the wicked is also indicated by a more accurate translation of the second part of verse 19. The Authorized Version has, "they are utterly consumed *with* terrors." The Hebrew original reads, "*from* terrors." Terrors are the source and cause of the destruction of the wicked. Terrors consume the wicked. These terrors are of all terrors the most fearsome: the infinite wrath of the righteous God avenging his offended holiness against the workers of iniquity. As the gracious God is the "portion" of the righteous (v. 26), so the just God is the destruction of the unrighteous.

Since God is the destroyer of the wicked, the destruction itself is the suffering of God's fiery wrath. The end of the wicked is damnation. Damned sinners experience destruction as all the pain of being wasted, caused to perish, and consumed by God, who is a "consuming fire" (Heb. 12:29). They experience destruction also as terrors: the boundless fears of guilty sinners at the awful absence of God in his goodness and at the equally awful nearness of God in his hatred. Their end is the black darkness of the absence of the gracious God, whose presence is life and joy. In this darkness, the wicked are afraid. In this darkness, God falls upon the wicked in his wrath. They are terrified. "It is a fearful thing to fall into the hands of the living God" (Heb. 10:31).

Everlasting Destruction

The destruction of the wicked is not their annihilation. They do not simply cease to exist. Just as the future life and glory of the children of God, promised in verses 23–26 of the psalm, are "for ever" (v. 26), so the future death and shame of the wicked are without end. Theirs is an endless end of destruction. That the destruction of the wicked is everlasting is implied in the dreadfulness of it. Nothingness does not answer to the dreadfulness of the end of the wicked in verses 18 and 19. Many wicked would not be terrified by the prospect of mere annihilation. Most would welcome this after a full, prosperous, earthly life of blaspheming God, despising his law, and persecuting his people. Only everlasting misery accounts for the dreadfulness of the end of the wicked, according to Psalm 73. The New Testament more fully declares that the destiny of the reprobate ungodly is everlasting torment in hell, body and soul: "It is better for thee to enter into life maimed, than having two hands to go into hell, into the fire that never shall be quenched: Where their worm dieth not, and the fire is not quenched" (Mark 9:43, 44).

Sudden Destruction

This terrible and terrifying destruction happens to all the wicked "as in a moment" (v. 19). Literally, the vivid Hebrew original has, "in a wink (or, blink) [of an eye]." Regardless whether an old reprobate dies in bed of old age at ninety, or a young reprobate dies violently in the prime of life, all are plunged suddenly from their prosperous earthly life into hell in the blink of an eye. Christ expresses this truth of the abruptness of the destruction of the wicked in the parable of the rich man and Lazarus: "the rich man also died, and was buried; And *in hell* he lift up his eyes" (Luke 16:22, 23). Their sudden destruction—the end of the wicked—hangs over the prosperous earthly life of every wicked man and every wicked woman like the sword of Damocles. The end, "in a blink of an eye," renders this prosperous life precarious, doomed, and unenviable.

This end is certain for all the wicked. God makes known in the sanctuary that destruction is their end. God has inspired the revelation in Psalm 73 of the end of all who live and die in unrighteousness. The psalmist doubted whether God curses the wicked in their life. He did not doubt that God curses them at their death.

How appalling is the end of the wicked! This was exactly the response of the psalmist to the end of the wicked, when he understood it in the sanctuary. At the beginning of verse 19, "how" is an exclamation of horror, as though the psalmist cried out, "Horror of horrors, they are brought into desolation, in a blink of an eye!"

Even if it were true that their brief, prosperous earthly life is a blessing in God's (common) grace, so dreadful is the end of the wicked that a Christian—indeed, anyone with good sense—would ignore their brief earthly blessing and concentrate on their everlasting cursedness.

But their earthly prosperity is no blessing, for their prosperous earthly life is related to their dreadful destruction. Their prosperity is the "slippery places" that send them sliding smoothly and swiftly through life unto their end of destruction. This connection between the dreadful end of the wicked and their preceding prosperous life is basic to the teaching of Psalm 73. Understanding the end of the wicked *in connection with the prosperous earthly life that brought them to this end,* the psalmist was delivered from the doubt that nearly brought about his spiritual fall—doubt whether God is good to Israel.

CHAPTER EIGHT

Slippery Places

*Surely thou didst set them in slippery places: thou castedst
them down into destruction.
How are they brought into desolation, as in a moment! they
are utterly consumed with terrors* (Ps. 73:18, 19).

Knowledge of the end
of the wicked—destruction, desolation, perishing, and being
consumed by terrors—delivered the psalmist from the temptation to envy their prosperous earthly life. For it is this very
prosperity that leads to their end. The end of the prosperous
wicked is not merely the cessation of their earthly life. Nor is
their end simply their everlasting destiny of woe. Rather, it is
the goal to which their prosperous life takes them. The prosperous life of the reprobate wicked has its natural, inevitable
end in eternal destruction, as a leisurely, pleasant boat ride
down the Niagara River has its end in a terrifying death in the
Falls.

For this reason it is a mistake, it is foolish, to evaluate the
prosperous life of the wicked apart from the end of this life.
This was the folly of the psalmist, for which he repented, ac-

cording to verses 21 and 22. This is also the folly of all propo-
nents of common grace, for which, however, they refuse to repent. They esteem the way—the prosperous earthly life of the
wicked—apart from the end of the way—destruction.

If it were not the case that their prosperity is the way to their
dreadful end, we might still envy the wicked. We might envy
their prosperous earthly life. The psalmist might suppose that,
although God will curse the wicked in eternity, he blesses them
in time. Likewise, although God will bless the psalmist in eternity, he fails to bless him in time. This was the psalmist's doubt,
as it is the great issue in Psalm 73: God is good to Israel *in time
and with regard to the circumstances of earthly life.*

Damning Prosperity

The prosperity of the wicked—their trouble-free lives, their
having more than heart could wish, their prospering in the
world, their increasing in riches—is to them "slippery places"
by which they go down swiftly and surely to eternal damnation. "Surely thou didst set them in slippery places: thou castedst them down into destruction" (v. 18). In the sanctuary, the
psalmist saw the prosperity of the wicked entirely differently
than he did before. Before, he saw it as enviable blessing. In the
sanctuary, he saw it as "slippery places...into destruction."

It is the nature of ease, comforts, pleasures, and riches to
dull the spiritual senses even of the godly with regard to the
truth of God, heavenly treasures, and judgment to come. How
much more does not prosperity blind and harden those who

are spiritually dead? If there were any hope at all for the wicked, it would be that earthly miseries—poverty, sickness, family troubles—would awaken them to the realities of a just God, his impending judgment, the brevity of this life, and a coming eternity. Prosperity makes those who are foolish to begin with, drunken. They are besotted with the enjoyment of earthly life apart from God. This is the figure Augustine used in his damning judgment of the prosperity of the wicked:

> There is no greater calamity than the happiness and prosperity of the ungodly; it is a strong wine which makes them drunk in their unrighteousness, and they incur thereby a huge amount and heavy load of God's wrath. [1]

Contrast this estimation of the prosperity of the wicked with the prevailing view that sees it as blessing!

Understanding that the prosperity of the wicked is "slippery places" unto the end of destruction, the psalmist was converted from his envy of the prosperity of the wicked. Who would envy, as a blessing, someone's sliding precipitously into hell?

The sliding of the wicked into destruction by their prosperity is God's doing. God gives prosperity to the reprobate wicked with the purpose that their prosperity ruins them eternally. By their prosperity God hardens the wicked in their care-

---

1. Quoted in Jean Taffin, *The Marks of God's Children*, trans. Peter Y. De Jong, ed. James A. De Jong (Grand Rapids, MI: Baker Academic, 2003), 127.

less, proud godlessness, so that they perish. This is the clear teaching of verse 18: "*Thou* didst set them in slippery places: *thou* castedst them down into destruction." This confession of God's sovereign destruction of the wicked in and by their earthly prosperity is prefaced with the emphatic, "Surely." About God's purpose and work of destruction with and in the prosperity of the wicked, there is no doubt.

Verse 18's confession of the sovereignty of God in the destruction of the wicked by means of their prosperity is too strong for many commentators. Even Joseph Addison Alexander, a Presbyterian, prefers to speak of God's *allowing* the wicked to plunge into destruction. This enables him to insist, in spite of the contrary teaching of the psalm, that the prosperity of the wicked is a grace of God to them. "[In Psalm 73:18, the psalmist] sees God, by his providential favours, placing them [the wicked] in this desired but fearful situation, and then allowing them to drop into destruction."[2]

D. Martyn Lloyd-Jones likewise quickly speaks of God's "permissive will": "We have to remember God's permissive will."[3] All the way through his rambling comment on verse 18, Lloyd-Jones insists on teaching that God merely withdraws some of his power that has been restraining the wicked and allows them to go their own way. "God has withdrawn His re-

---

2. Joseph Addison Alexander, *The Psalms Translated and Explained* (Grand Rapids, MI: Baker, 1975), 309.

3. D. Martyn Lloyd-Jones, *Faith on Trial* (Grand Rapids, MI: Eerdmans, 1965), 55.

straining power. He has allowed sin to develop and reveal it-self for what it really is."[4]

However, the language of the inspired text rejects all such weakening of the doctrine. God puts the wicked in slippery places, obviously with the purpose that they *slide*—slide *into destruction*. The second part of verse 18 uses what is known in Hebrew grammar as the Hiphil stem of the verb, *to fall* (rightly translated as "castedst...down" by the Authorized Version). The Hiphil stem of Hebrew verbs often expresses divine sovereignty. It teaches that God *causes* this or that event. Such is the case in the second part of verse 18. A literal translation would be: "Thou didst cause them to fall into destruction."

Their prosperity is God's way of destroying the prosperous wicked. It is not merely the case, although this would be bad enough, that their prosperity in fact contributes to their damnation because they misuse it and are unthankful for it. This is indeed true, but it is not the teaching of verse 18. The teaching of the text is that God gives the wicked their prosperity in order to accomplish and ensure their destruction. The present earthly prosperity of the wicked is itself divine destruction of the wicked inasmuch as it hastens them to final destruction.

The thought of verse 18 is this: O God, whose goodness to Israel I once doubted, because I foolishly supposed that the prosperity of the wicked is thy blessing of them, I now under-

4. Ibid., 60.

stand that with this prosperity and by this prosperity thou dost set the wicked in slippery places, so that they slide smoothly, swiftly, and surely into destruction.

Implied is God's sovereign reprobation of these wicked in his eternal decree of predestination. In the same decree in which he elected Israel to salvation in the way of their cleansing their hearts and washing their hands, he appointed these wicked persons to damnation in the way of the slippery places of prosperity. If in history God sets men and women in slippery places in order that they slide into eternal damnation, he does so according to an eternal purpose that they not be saved in Jesus Christ, but perish on account of their wickedness.

Unenviable Prosperity

Who will envy the prosperity of the wicked now? The farm upon which the sun always shines and the rain always falls in season? The popularity of the beautiful movie starlet? The fame of the gifted athlete? The wealth of the business tycoon? The comfortable life of the next door neighbor, without a care in the world?

Who will suppose that this prosperity is a blessing, a gracious gift of God to the wicked in his love?

Who will now suppose that it is better to be unrighteous than to be holy *with regard to the circumstances of earthly life?*

In light of the truth about the prosperity of the wicked, will we Christians not also view our own earthly life of troubles differently than we did before, when we envied the prosperity of the wicked? Will we not now view our life of plagues and chastisements as leading us to our end of glory? Will we not now view our troubles as blessings, as the unfailing goodness of God to us?

One question remains with regard to the prosperous earthly life of the wicked in light of the end of this life: What is God's attitude toward the prosperous earthly life of the ungodly? Is he as impressed with it as are the prosperous ungodly themselves? Is he as impressed with it as are those theologians who attribute this prosperous life to the grace of God? Is God's attitude toward the prosperous ungodly one of favor? This question the psalmist answers in verse 20.

CHAPTER NINE

Held in Divine Contempt

As a dream when one awaketh; so, O Lord, when thou awakest,
thou shalt despise their image (Ps. 73:20).

MISUNDERSTANDING
of the attitude of God toward the prosperous ungodly was part
of the psalmist's spiritual struggle. He supposed that God has a
favorable attitude toward the ungodly who prosper in the
world, that God is gracious to them. If the prosperity of the
wicked is divine blessing of them, as the psalmist thought, then
the attitude of God whence this blessing comes is favor, or
grace. This would imply that the earthly troubles of the godly
are the manifestation of divine disfavor, that is, wrath, toward
afflicted Israel.

The attitude of God toward the prosperous ungodly is implied by their end. Their end is destruction. To this end, God
ordained these wicked in his decree. This end he caused them
to reach by loading them with riches and ease in his providential government of their earthly lives. "Surely thou didst set
them in slippery places: thou castedst them down into de-

struction" (v. 18). God hates these prosperous wicked. He regards them as loathsome. He wills their misery of destruction, desolation, and utter consumption as just punishment of their wickedness. Although their end makes the divine hatred known, God does not begin to hate them only at their end. Rather, the end reveals what God's attitude toward them was all along. Throughout their prosperous earthly lives, God was setting them in slippery places.

God's Despising

If the attitude of God toward the prosperous wicked is implied by their end, it is stated explicitly in verse 20: "Thou shalt despise their image."

Whatever the image of the wicked may be, in despising the image of the wicked God despises the wicked themselves. Their image is themselves in a certain respect. Despising their image, God despises them. This adds something to the divine hatred of the prosperous wicked. God holds them in contempt. He regards them as despicable, shameful creatures.

What a contrast with their appearance in life! They seem to be glorious men and women: rich, successful, powerful. What a contrast with their own estimation of themselves! They adorn themselves with pride as a necklace (v. 6). What a contrast with the high regard for them on the part of their fellow men! So impressed with the prosperous wicked are the masses that many of them idolize these wicked men and women, adopt their thinking, and follow their ways (v. 10). What a contrast with the view of the prosperous wicked the children of God have in our weaker moments! With the psalmist, we envy them (v. 3).

But God despises the prosperous wicked.

God's attitude is right. These people are contemptible. Mere creatures, living by God's providential power, enjoying the prosperity he gives them, they boast of themselves and speak blasphemies against God.

God's despising of the prosperous wicked is an *effectual* attitude of disdain. He puts them to shame. Death is shameful. Hell is the place of shame, as well as of torment.

Again, although God fully discloses his attitude and executes it in the punishment of the prosperous wicked at the end, such was his attitude all along. They never impressed God with all their wealth, ease, and pomp. Much less did God regard these proud, unthankful, blaspheming sinners as honorable.

That God despised the ungodly when they were in the peak of their earthly splendor is indicated by the psalmist's description of their earthly life of prosperity and power as merely an "image": "Thou shalt despise their image." We must not think of the image of God (which the ungodly do not have) or of the image of the devil (which they have) or even of some resemblance of the wicked.

"Image" in verse 20 must be understood in connection with the phrase, "as a dream when one awaketh." When someone wakes up of a morning, he may have a faint, shadowy memory of a dream he had while sleeping. This faint, fleeting memory is the meaning of "image" in verse 20. This is all that the prosperous earthly life of the ungodly amounts to. It is not even comparable to a dream itself, which, in fact, is nothing. But the prosperous life of the ungodly is comparable to the faint *memory* of a dream.

The life of the prosperous ungodly is a mere image. It is without substance. It is empty and worthless, as empty and worthless as a faint memory of a dream. There is nothing to it. "Image" as the description of the prosperous life of the wicked, explains Calvin, expresses "that all which we gaze at in this world is nothing else than pure vanity."[1] The life of the prosperous ungodly, therefore, is unenviable. Who in his right mind envies an image?

The prosperous earthly life of the wicked is a mere image because it is human life lived without God and his blessing and because it ends in destruction in a very short time.

A mere image is what the life of the prosperous wicked is in the judgment of God. As such, this life is despised by him. He despises the people who live such a life. But he also despises the life itself. It is the prosperous earthly life of the wicked that is the object of the divine contempt in verse 20: "Thou shalt despise their *image*." God's attitude with regard to the prosperity of the wicked is not favor, but contempt.

God's Sleeping

God reveals his attitude toward the prosperous earthly life of the ungodly and fully executes his attitude "when thou awak-

1. John Calvin, *Commentary on the Book of Psalms*, vol. 2, trans. James Anderson (Grand Rapids, MI: Baker, 1998), 147.

est." Verse 20 speaks of a strange awakening of God. For a time, he sleeps. Finally, he wakes up. With regard to the individual, God wakes up at the moment of the end of every wicked man or woman. This, as we have seen, refers to the death of the wicked as the beginning of their destruction. Before this, during the earthly life of the wicked, God sleeps. With regard to the ungodly race, God wakes up on the day of Christ, when he judges the world in righteousness. During history he sleeps, or at least dozes off.

Scripture mentions God's awakening elsewhere. Psalm 44: 23 calls on God to awake in view of the persecution of his people: "Awake, why sleepest thou, O Lord? arise, cast us not off for ever." God's waking up is a figurative way of teaching his seeming inactivity in punishing the wicked who oppress the church, and redeeming his people who suffer grievously. In reality, God is not inactive regarding the judging of the wicked prior to their end. He sets them in slippery places. Neither is God oblivious to the suffering of his people. He upholds them in their suffering and makes it serve their eternal glory. "Behold, he that keepeth Israel shall neither slumber nor sleep" (Ps. 121:4).

But it seems to us that he sleeps. The wicked prosper and vaunt themselves. The righteous are plagued. Only at the end both of the prosperous wicked and of the plagued righteous does God awake, destroying the wicked and delivering the righteous.

The figure of God's sleeping and waking is striking, powerful, and even daring. Underlying the figure and accounting for its use is a fundamental truth about the nature and works of God. This truth is that God is good to his Israel, and to Israel only. Any apparent evil to Israel and all apparent good to the ungodly can only be explained in terms of God's sleeping. God has fallen asleep on the job. Rather this explanation of the seeming blessing of the ungodly and lack of blessing of the clean of heart than the explanation that God does indeed bless the wicked and curse his people! Better that God temporarily neglects to perform his proper works of blessing his church and cursing his enemies than that he deliberately goes back on his word of promise!

In fact, he does not neglect to perform his proper works. He does not fall asleep in time and history, when the wicked prosper and the righteous are plagued. With regard both to the reprobate wicked and to his elect Israel, he works in the earthly circumstances of their lives with a view to their end. The wicked he sets in slippery places, so that they slide into destruction. His children he chastens, so that they inherit glory. God is wide awake in history. God is wide awake in the earthly life of each one of his people.

There are good reasons why God seemingly sleeps, so that the wicked prosper in the world. In many ways, the prosperous wicked serve God's purposes. As far as Psalm 73 is concerned, there is one reason why the wicked prosper as God "sleeps." The prosperity of the wicked, in contrast with our own troubles, tests our faith that God is good to Israel. We must believe that God is good to Israel, simply on the basis of God's own promise in Jesus Christ, crucified and risen. We must believe his goodness, even though we neither see nor feel it. We must believe his goodness to us, the clean of heart, even though the testimony of our physical senses is that he is good, not to us, but to his enemies, who blaspheme him and ridicule us.

With regard to the circumstances of our everyday, earthly life, we are called to live by faith, not by sight. With regard to the circumstances of earthly life, we are saved by faith. And this faith by which we are saved looks intently and expectantly to the end. Faith takes form as hope. Thus, "we are saved by hope: but hope that is seen is not hope: for what a man seeth, why doth he yet hope for? But if we hope for that we see not, then do we with patience wait for it" (Rom. 8:24, 25).

CHAPTER TEN

Beastly Folly

*Thus my heart was grieved, and I was pricked in my reins.
So foolish was I, and ignorant: I was as a beast
before thee* (Ps. 73: 21, 22).

Penitance IN keeping with the experiential nature of the psalms, the entire seventy-third psalm bares the soul of the psalmist to us regarding his fearful struggle with a powerful temptation. The psalmist was tempted to suppose that God is not good to the clean of heart in the circumstances of their earthly lives, but that he is good to the wicked. Verses 21 and 22 disclose the psalmist's present sorrow of soul over his former sin of yielding to the temptation. Verse 21 describes the psalmist's repentance after he learned the end of the wicked, in the sanctuary of God. The sin of which he repents is acknowledged in verse 22: "So foolish was I."

Verses 21 and 22 are not a further description of the psalmist's wicked feelings and passions during the time he was envious of the wicked, as is commonly supposed and as the Authorized Version's unfortunate translation of verse 21 suggests.

Verse 21 expresses deep sorrow. The psalmist's heart is "grieved," and he is "pricked," or "pierced through"—as is the Hebrew original—in his reins. The psalmist does not describe his past experience when he was envying the wicked and doubting God's goodness to himself. Rather, he describes his present experience after he went into the sanctuary of God and there learned the truth about the earthly prosperity of the wicked. His sorrow is not the evil passion of envy, but the good, healthy grief of penitence. The grief of the psalmist is the sorrow of true repentance over his sin.

There is evidence that the grief spoken of in verse 21 is godly sorrow over sin. First, the language itself proves this: a grieved heart and pierced, or wounded, reins. The psalms do not use this language to describe the sinful passions of the child of God. A grieving, suffering heart and pained reins may refer either to the experience of sore affliction or to the experience of repentance. The latter is plainly in view in verse 21.

Second, the grammar of the Hebrew original is decisive for understanding the grief as the sorrow of repentance. Both of the verbs in verse 21 occur in the imperfect inflection, not the perfect inflection. Nor are they converted into the perfect inflection by the special use of the conjunction, *waw*. Verbs in the imperfect inflection are to be translated either as futures or as continuous presents. They are not to be translated in the past tense, as the Authorized Version translates the two verbs: "*was* grieved" and "*was* pricked." In verse 21, the two verbs must be translated as continuous presents: "my heart is continuously grieved, and I am continuously pierced in my reins." The experience of grief of heart and the feeling of woundedness in his reins are the present spiritual condition of the psalmist.

What the psalmist learned in the sanctuary was not merely academic. The truth of the word of God worked conversion in him, consisting of a deep-seated and thorough-going repentance. The psalmist's heart is bitter with sorrow over his sin. This affects his feelings, associated in the Hebrew mind with the reins, or kidneys.

The Sin of Foolish Thinking

The sin concerning which the psalmist experienced the grief of repentance was his past envy at the foolish because of their earthly prosperity, and his past doubt of the goodness of God to him in the circumstances of his life because of his troubles. The sin over which he now repents is referred to in verse 22: "So foolish was I, and ignorant: I was as a beast before thee." The Authorized Version correctly uses the past tense of the verb in verse 22: "I *was* as a beast." In verse 22 the perfect inflection occurs, which is usually translated as a past tense. The thought is this: "When I envied the prosperous ungodly, thinking that God blessed them in his favor, and when I supposed that God dealt with me in his disfavor because of all my earthly troubles, I was as a beast."

The psalmist's former thinking about the prosperity of the wicked and about the troubles of the children of God was sin.

It was not merely a misunderstanding, a mental mistake, or an intellectual error. The psalmist repents of that thinking; he repents with deep, keenly felt sorrow.

It is particularly the folly of his sinful thinking about the prosperity of the wicked that grieves the psalmist: "So foolish was I." The psalmist lacked the sound understanding of a human. He was "as a beast." That thinking is sound which is in accordance with the truth of God as revealed in his word. Regarding the circumstances of the earthly lives of men and women, sound thinking is that which harmonizes with God's revelation that he is good—always and only good—to Israel, to the clean of heart. But the thinking of the psalmist contradicted the word of God. This was folly. This was the stupidity of a beast.

We must be perfectly clear about thinking that is condemned as so foolish that a professing Christian who thinks such foolishness is more like an animal than a man. It is the thinking that God is good to the wicked in his grace when he gives them earthly prosperity. It is the thinking that God is *not* good to his children—to *me*—when he sends earthly troubles of all kinds. The thinking confessed by the psalmist to be folly is the same folly today called common grace: God is gracious to the wicked and ungracious to his people in the circumstances of their earthly lives; the prosperity of the ungodly is a temporal blessing, whereas the troubles of the godly are a temporal curse.

This thinking about earthly prosperity and earthly troubles is not theological wisdom, but spiritual folly. The thinker must not flatter himself that he is a sharp theologian, but must humble himself as beast-like in his foolishness.

Such thinking is sinfully foolish. The psalmist repents of this thinking because he sinned against God. By this thinking, he corrupted the truth of the righteous God, as though God can love, be gracious to, and bless blaspheming, depraved sinners apart from the satisfying of his justice in the cross of Christ. The psalmist's thinking was unbelief, as though God, having given his Son for his beloved Israel, can withhold from his people the lesser blessing of his goodness in the earthly circumstances of their lives, and even treat them hurtfully in wrath.

For theologians and others in the New Testament age to entertain and promote such thinking about the prosperity of the wicked and the troubles of the saints is worse sin than it was for the psalmist. New Testament theologians have the clear instruction of Psalm 73 that the prosperity of the wicked is "slippery places" on which the wicked slide to destruction. They have the comforting word of God in Romans 8:32: "He that spared not his own Son, but delivered him up for us all, how shall he not with him also freely give us all things?"

The theology of a common grace of God is folly. No Reformed seminary may teach it. No minister may preach it. No Christian may defend it. All who are guilty of thinking and teaching this theology must repent of their sin. The doctrine of common grace is not the truth of the gospel about the circumstances of earthly life. It deceives the prosperous wicked. It distresses the afflicted child of God. It corrupts the revelation of God. This is the testimony of Psalm 73, particularly verses 21 and 22.

Nevertheless, we believers are prone to this foolish thinking. Again and again, when troubles fall on our faithful churches, on God's holy people, and especially on ourselves while unfaithful churches prosper, the wicked live trouble-free lives, and our ungodly neighbor goes from strength to strength, we find ourselves thinking the foolish thoughts exposed in Psalm 73. The reason is our natural ignorance. "So foolish was I," the psalmist confesses in verse 22 and adds, in explanation of his folly, "and ignorant." In ourselves, according to our corrupt nature, we are spiritually ignorant, ready to attribute the prosperity of the wicked to God's love for them and our own troubles to a lack of love toward us.

The only safeguard against this foolish thinking all our lives long is the word of God. His word is this: "Truly God is good to Israel."

CHAPTER ELEVEN

Kept from Falling

Nevertheless I am continually with thee: thou hast holden me by my right hand (Ps. 73:23).

THE contrast in verse 23, correctly picked up by the "nevertheless" of the Authorized Version, is between the psalmist's present, indeed, continual covenant fellowship with God, on the one hand, and his past sinful stupidity of envying the prosperous wicked and doubting God's goodness to himself, on the other hand. In his foolish unbelief, he departed from God. He deserved to be cast away by God. But he finds, to his amazement, that he is still "with thee."

God has converted the psalmist in the sanctuary (v. 17), so that he has repented of his sin and confessed it (vv. 21, 22). Penitent, he is forgiven and reconciled to God. But now the psalmist sees that he was "with thee" even in the time of his miserable unbelief: "continually with thee," he says. The psalmist departed from God, but he did not entirely fall away from God.

There has been indication in the preceding verses that the

psalmist was "with thee" even when he envied the foolish and doubted the goodness of God to the clean of heart. For one thing, verse 2 recounted that the feet of the psalmist were *"almost* gone" and that his steps "had *well nigh* slipped." In fact, his feet did not go, neither did his steps slip. For another thing, in his worst moments, when he concluded that it was useless to serve God, the psalmist could not utter this blasphemy for fear of offending God's children (v. 15). There remained in him a love for God's people, reflecting, however faintly, a love for God. Then also, he still went into the sanctuary (v. 17). He kept the first table of the law of God. He went to church, regardless of the fact that he had to drag himself there.

The Preservation of a Saint

Verses 23 and 24 explain this perseverance of the psalmist. In these verses is a testimony to the wonderful, preserving grace of God in the life of the foolish, doubting child of God. This grace shines brightly against the dark background of the psalmist's own sin, which he confessed in verses 21 and 22. It is the grace of God's faithfulness to the psalmist when the psalmist was unfaithful to God.

This faithfulness of God is covenant faithfulness. "With thee" affirms the unbroken and unbreakable covenant between God and the psalmist. "With" in Scripture is the covenant preposition. The psalmist is in communion with God by that living, spiritual bond in which God is the psalmist's God and the psalmist is God's servant, son, and friend.

The psalmist has always been with God. He was with God even when he doubted God's goodness to himself in the circumstances of his earthly life and nearly despaired of the worth of a holy life in the covenant. The psalmist was not conscious of his communion with God when he doubted and despaired. He did not enjoy this communion. But the bond established by God in the circumcising of the psalmist's heart never broke. Although the psalmist on his part forsook God, God on his part remained close to the psalmist.

"Nevertheless," the converted child of God cries out in verse 23, "despite my un-covenantal and anti-covenantal unbelief, I am now, and have always been, with thee."

What a contrast to the life of the prosperous ungodly! For all their prosperity, they were never with God. As verse 27 states, they were always "far from thee."

The sole explanation why the psalmist is yet, and always remained, in covenant communion with God is that God held him by his right hand: "Thou hast holden me by my right hand" (v. 23). This holding is the power of the grace of God in Jesus Christ. Obviously, the holding is a saving power. It kept the psalmist's feet from going and his steps from slipping. It is the power of the preservation of the psalmist from apostasy and damnation as described in the Canons of Dordt, V, 6:

> But God, who is rich in mercy, according to his unchangeable purpose of election, does not wholly withdraw the Holy Spirit from his own people, even in their melancholy falls; nor suffer them to proceed so

far as to lose the grace of adoption and forfeit the state
of justification, or to commit the sin unto death; nor
does he permit them to be totally deserted, and to
plunge themselves into everlasting destruction.[1]

God's holding is the power of the conversion of the psalmist in
the sanctuary as described in the Canons, V, 7:

> By his Word and Spirit, he [God] certainly and effectu-
> ally renews them [God's greatly sinning people] to re-
> pentance, to a sincere and godly sorrow for their sins,
> that they may seek and obtain remission in the blood
> of the Mediator, may again experience the favor of a
> reconciled God, through faith adore his mercies, and
> henceforward more diligently work out their own sal-
> vation with fear and trembling.[2]

The holding of the psalmist by God is also a power of tender love. God held him, the psalmist exclaims in wonderment,
"by my right hand" (v. 23). As a father securely holds a stumbling little son in the grip of love, so God held the hand of his
slipping child.

This powerful, loving holding is covenant preservation.
The psalmist was "with thee," and he was with God because

---

1. Canons of Dordtrecht, V, 6, in Philip Schaff, ed., *Creeds of Christendom*, vol.
3 (1931; reprint, Grand Rapids, MI: Baker, 1998), 593.
2. Canons of Dordt, V, 7, in Schaff, *Creeds of Christendom*, vol. 3, 594.

God was with him. So close was the communion that God walked hand in hand with him.

"Thou hast holden me"!

Every one of us who believes in God through Jesus Christ looks back on some dark time in our life, when we stumbled, and we exclaim, "Thou didst hold me." Every one of us looks back on a time when, like the psalmist, we doubted the goodness of God because of the hard circumstances of our life, and we cry out, "Thou didst hold me."

God held us. We did not hold on to God. Stupidly, we let go of God in our envy and doubt. The continuation of the covenant with us is gracious, not conditional. And inasmuch as we did not entirely let go of God—and we did not—that was because God held us, not allowing us to let go of him altogether.

What a contrast between the life of the psalmist and the life of the prosperous wicked! God held up the psalmist as a father holds up his dear child so that the child will not fall. God set the wicked in slippery places *so that* they will fall, as a just judge executes sentence against the guilty. To Israel, his covenant friends, God is good. To his enemies, he is terrible.

CHAPTER TWELVE

The End of the Troubled Saints

*Thou shalt guide me with thy counsel, and afterward
receive me to glory* (Ps. 73: 24).

THE truth that God held him
in the time of his severe spiritual struggle, the time of his doubt
of and departure from God, arouses in the psalmist the confidence that God will guide him all the rest of his life on earth:
"Thou shalt guide me." God's guidance is his care for and di-
rection of the entire earthly lives of his covenant people, Israel.
In this guidance, God carefully arranges all the circumstances
of the psalmist's life. In this guidance, God will also lead the
psalmist spiritually, so that he will not again doubt God's goodness, but, as the psalmist declares in verse 28, will put his trust
in the Lord GOD. The psalmist has been cured of his wicked
belief of common grace for the ungodly and common wrath for
the godly.

This guidance is personal: "guide *me.*" In the tender love of
a father, God not only has a care for the covenant people as a
body, but also for each of the members of the body individu-

ally. Not only does God direct the history of the church, but he also directs the life of each elect child of God.

The Guiding Counsel

That with which God guides the earthly life of each of his children is his counsel. The psalmist does not speak of God's word, or law. The reference, therefore, is not to the rule, or standard, of a holy life to which the psalmist actively conforms. The subject is not the truth of God's guidance of his people by making known to them his will for their lives. God does guide his people in this way, but this is not the thought of the text.

The guidance in view in verse 24 takes place by God's counsel. The Hebrew word translated "counsel" refers to God's eternal plan, or decree. It is the word used in Isaiah 46:10: "My counsel shall stand, and I will do all my pleasure." The text in Isaiah teaches that God's counsel is sovereign. He forms it as pleases him, not in dependency on any other. He also executes it to the last detail. Nothing that he has planned fails to happen exactly as he planned it in history. God's counsel is his eternal decree ordaining all that takes place in time and history. Specifically, in verse 24, it is God's plan for the entire earthly life of the psalmist. This plan is subservient in the counsel to God's election of the psalmist unto salvation. God's plan for the earthly life of the psalmist is controlled by the psalmist's election in Christ Jesus.

The earthly life of the child of God is not the product of blind historical development. Nor are the difficulties in the life of the child of God due to God's forgetting him, or to God's temporarily dealing with him in wrath and curse. Rather, all the life of the child of God is decreed. It is decreed by the will that chose him in Christ with such a love as gave Jesus Christ to the cross for him. In this way may—and must—the child of God view and receive the painful circumstances that tempt him to doubt God's goodness to him. It should come as no surprise to the child of God that his life is mysterious, beyond figuring out. It is the product of the deep wisdom of the incomprehensible God.

The notion that earthly life, with its circumstances of prosperity for the wicked and adversity for the godly, must be divorced from the counsel of predestination is false. This notion prevails among professing Calvinists, to say nothing of all those who outrightly deny predestination. This is the notion that, in violent contradiction of his counsel's appointing some to destruction in hatred for them, God loves these reprobate in history and blesses them with prosperity and ease. Implied is the notion that, in equally violent contradiction of his counsel's appointing the elect to salvation in love for them, God treats his chosen people ungraciously in time in that he grievously afflicts them. In the language of Psalm 73, it is the notion that, although God will be terrible to the ungodly at their end, he is good to them during their earthly lives. Although God will be good to the clean of heart "afterward," he is not good to them in the here and now. Thus, the notion, popular as it is, flatly contradicts the theme of Psalm 73: "Truly God is good to Israel."

The truth is that God guides the earthly lives of his chosen people by his counsel. In harmony with his counsel, he guides their lives. His counsel determines their earthly lives.

According to his counsel, centered on our election, God sends us afflictions in grace, as a blessing and for our good. According to his counsel, centered on their reprobation, God sends the ungodly prosperity in wrath, as a curse and for their damnation.

By God's counsel, we are guided. By God's counsel, the ungodly are cast down to destruction.

Guided to Glory

Guidance, or leading, implies a goal, a destiny, an end. God will guide the psalmist to a certain end. The second part of verse 24, "and afterward receive me to glory," teaches that there is an end, or destiny, to which God guides the psalmist and what that end is.

"Afterward" corresponds to the "end" of the wicked in verse 17. As the prosperous wicked have their end, so the plagued and chastened children of God have their "afterward." Like the "end" of the wicked, the "afterward" of the children of God refers to the everlasting destiny reached at the instant of physical death. As with the ungodly, so also with the godly, this earthly life is not all there is to existence. Death is not annihilation for the righteous or for the wicked. At the moment death concludes this earthly life, "afterward," righteous and wicked alike reach their end.

How radically different, however, are the end of the wicked and the end of the saints! The end of the wicked is destruction. The end of the psalmist, which God has proposed for him in his counsel, will be "glory." In verse 23 the psalmist has expressed the confidence that his end will be everlasting life, for he is certain that he is "continually with thee [God]." To be with God is life. It is the rich, joyful life of the covenant. The psalmist has this life already during his earthly pilgrimage. Now that he is delivered from his sinful doubts about God's goodness to him, he also enjoys this life of fellowship with God. This life is everlasting: "I am *continually* with thee" (v. 23). Death cannot destroy it or even interrupt it. The covenant of God with his chosen people in Christ is everlasting. The end of the psalmist will be that he continues to be with God, that is, that he lives. His end will not be mere continued existence, but life. Afterward, he will enjoy this spiritual life without any hindrance of trouble, sin, and death.

But the end of the psalmist will not only be life. It will also be glory. The psalmist will share in the splendor of the radiating beauty and honor of the God of all perfections, who alone is glorious. A higher, better, worthier, more desirable destiny for a human is inconceivable. God himself can give his children no greater good. Implied is that the end of the wicked is not only torment, but also shame. Implied also is that in earthly life the children of God endure shame for God's sake. Glory comes "afterward."

Glory is the *end* of the children of God in the sense that it is the *goal* of all God's guidance throughout our earthly lives.

Certainly glory as our end is a future reward that will far out-weigh all our present suffering and shame. "For I reckon that the sufferings of this present time are not worthy to be com-pared with the glory which shall be revealed in us" (Rom. 8:18). But glory is also the destiny being worked out for us by means of the present suffering, the plaguing and chastening of Psalm 73:14. Our present chastisement is related to the future glory, as the present prosperity of the wicked is related to their com-ing destruction. As the slippery slide of prosperity plunges the wicked into hell, so the uphill climb of the troubles of the Christian's life brings him, by God's guidance, to heaven and its glory.

In the sanctuary, the psalmist understood the end of the prosperous wicked (v. 17), and he understood that the pros-perity of the wicked brings them to this end. Therefore, he learned the truth about the prosperity of the wicked. It is noth-ing but "slippery places" (v. 18). The prosperity of the wicked is not to be envied. Neither is it God's blessing of the wicked.

In the sanctuary, the psalmist understood another great truth as well. This great truth is the end of the godly. He un-derstood what this end is—glorious life—and he understood that the troubles of the godly bring them to this end. This is the message, the grand gospel message, of Psalm 73. The mes-sage of Psalm 73 is not simply that present troubles will be fol-lowed by future glory. The message of Psalm 73 is not even that present troubles will be outweighed by future glory. But the message of Psalm 73 is that the present troubles are the neces-sary way to the future glory. Without the troubles there can be no glory. The troubles themselves realize the future glory. The truth about the troubles of the godly, particularly himself, that recovered the stumbling feet and slipping steps of the psalmist was the doctrine stated in 2 Corinthians 4:17: "Our light affliction, which is but for a moment, worketh for us a far more exceeding and eternal weight of glory."

Israel's earthly troubles do not conflict with God's promise to be good to his covenant people. Much less are they manifestations of his disfavor toward the clean of heart, as they must be if prosperity and ease are gracious blessing. The troubles of the righteous are the *expressions* of God's favor toward his children as he guides them infallibly to the glorious end he has ordained for them. Just as there is no reason to be envious of the prosperity of the wicked, so there is no reason for the afflicted saint to be doubtful or even bitter concerning his poverty, sickness, family troubles, disappointments, and persecutions.

How our earthly troubles work out for us the end of glory is abundantly evident in everyday earthly life, in Scripture, and in our own spiritual experience. In everyday earthly life, the disciplined child grows up to healthy maturity, whereas the spoiled child, whose parents indulge his every wish and never chastise, becomes nothing but a grown up child. Scripture testifies that divine chastisements, *painful* divine chastisements, turn us from sin to God, take our hearts off the earth and its pleasures, wrench our affections from this fading life and its perishing treasures, and cause us to seek the inheritance laid away for us with Christ in heaven. Regarding our own experience, never do we search our lives for sin, never do we humble ourselves, never do we confess our sinfulness and transgressions, never do we seek God in prayer, never do we renounce our own strength for the strength of the Holy Spirit, never do we plead for mercy, never do we break with every evil way, as we do in the hour of great trouble. God's discipline not only guides us to the end of glory, but also increases in us the capacity to receive and enjoy that glory.

Glory "Afterward"

The holy children of God arrive at glory "afterward," that is, immediately upon the ending of earthly life at the instant of death. In view of the fuller light of the New Testament, we distinguish two phases of the glory that will be ours afterward. The first phase will be glory in the soul at once upon dying. Of this, Revelation 20:4 testifies: "I saw the souls of them that were beheaded for the witness of Jesus, and for the word of God...and they lived and reigned with Christ a thousand years." In his soul, the child of God lives with Christ—*consciously* lives with Christ—immediately upon dying. But he also reigns with Christ upon a throne. This is glory.

The second phase will be glory in soul and body at the resurrection of the dead in the day of Christ. "Who [the Lord Jesus Christ] shall change our vile body, that it may be fashioned like unto his glorious body, according to the working whereby he is able even to subdue all things unto himself" (Phil. 3:21).

The Old Testament does not so sharply distinguish the two phases of glory, at least not in Psalm 73. It only speaks of "afterward...glory." But the Old Testament does promise a glorious future life on the other side of death. It promises glory, and glory only. It promises glory endlessly.

We arrive at this end of glory, because afterward God *takes* us to glory. "Receive" in verse 24 has the sense of *take*: "and afterward *take* me to glory." God does not passively receive us to glory, that is, allow us to have glory upon our actively bringing ourselves to the glory. Instead, having actively guided us throughout our earthly life, God actively, indeed by a miracle, takes us to glory. He takes us to glory in our soul at the moment of death. He takes us to glory in our body and soul by raising our body from the grave and reuniting body and soul.

Of this, the psalmist was certain. He was certain of final glory for himself personally: "afterward receive me to glory." The psalmist doubted God's goodness to him in the circumstances of life. He did not doubt his future glory. Assurance of future glory and therefore of personal salvation is the normal experience of every child of God. God gives this assurance to all his children with the gift of faith. The miserable teaching that many, if not most, of God's believing children must live much, if not all, of their life doubting whether God will receive them to glory, *and that God wants it so,* is false doctrine. The Holy Spirit exposes the error in verse 24. With confidence every covenant friend of God says, "Thou shalt...afterward receive me to glory." Only in this confidence of our end can we rightly understand and bear our present trouble.

We must view and receive our present troubles in light of our glorious end. Never may we look away from our end, from the "afterward." If we take our eye of faith and hope off the coming glory, we will stumble and slip on account of the present, grievous evils in our life. Looking intently to the end, we will be able to bear the evils. We will even be able to rejoice in our afflictions, inasmuch as they work our glory. They are blessings.

CHAPTER THIRTEEN

God Our Only Good

*Whom have I in heaven but thee? and there is none upon earth
that I desire beside thee.
My flesh and my heart faileth: but God is the strength of my heart,
and my portion for ever* (Ps. 73:25, 26).

The Only Good in Heaven

IN the question, "Whom have I in heaven?" (the words "but thee," inserted by the translators of the Authorized Version, are not in the Hebrew original), the child of God expresses that God is to him the only good, so that the only reason that heaven is desirable is that God is there. The thought of heaven arises because the psalmist has just declared, "afterward [thou shalt] receive me to glory" (v. 24). Heaven is the place where he will receive and enjoy glory. What makes heaven heaven is God, who dwells there. Heaven will be heaven for the psalmist, because there, being with God in the perfection of the fellowship of the covenant, he will possess and enjoy God to the fullest.

The thought of having God in the communion of the covenant is in the text. The literal translation of the second part of verse 25 is, "and *with* thee I have not desired [anything] on earth." The translation, *"beside* thee," in the Authorized Version is mistaken. The word in the Hebrew original is the same word that occurs in verse 23 and is there correctly translated "with thee": "I am continually with thee." In the fellowship of the covenant, God gives himself to the member of Israel, to the one who is clean of heart, so that God is with his covenant friend and the covenant friend is with God. God gives himself to his friend as the only good. In this communion, God's covenant friend knows and desires God as the only good. Living with God as the only good climaxes in heaven.

For this reason, heaven is desirable to the psalmist. Heaven is not desirable because of its bliss and glory. Heaven is not even desirable because it is deliverance from the pains of hell. But heaven is desirable because there God is and there we have God. Without the presence of God, heaven is of no interest to the child of God. As that which makes a house a delightful home to a child is the presence of good, beloved parents, so that which makes heaven delightful is being with God.

The Only Good on Earth

Likewise, God is our only delight on earth. The thought of the second part of verse 25 is very forceful, because the truth expressed is radical: There is nothing and no one on earth who we have delighted in. Literally, the second part of verse 25 reads: "And with thee I have not desired on earth." In heaven there is nothing but God, and on earth there is nothing but

God, *as the object of our delight and desire.* God, to us, is the only good.

The truth is not merely that we delight *more* in God than in other persons and things. Plainly, the truth is that we delight in God alone. We do not delight in and thus desire earthly riches and comforts, power, a name, food and drink, friends, family, health, or earthly life itself. None of these things by itself is the good. All of these things together are not the good. Therefore, they are not precious to us. Since they are not precious, we do not delight in them. The truth expressed in verse 25 is perfectly captured in the versification of the Psalter, number 203: "And, having Thee, on earth is nought / That I can yet desire."[1]

God is the good. He is the totality of all perfections, and infinitely so. He is beautiful in grace, lovely in mercy, adorable in truth, awesome in holiness, splendid in righteousness, and grand in power.

Our Only Good

As the good, God is ours: "my portion" (v. 26). One's portion is an inheritance that comes to him. We do not delight in him from afar. He is the riches of our inheritance. God has given himself to us in the intimate fellowship of his covenant, so that

---

1. No. 203, third stanza in *The Psalter with Doctrinal Standards, Liturgy, Church Order, and Added Chorale Section,* revised ed. (Grand Rapids, MI: Eerdmans, 1995), 171.

all his goodness is ours, as a father wills himself and all his possessions to his children. "With thee," according to the Hebrew original, "I have not desired on earth." That is, "Living with thee in the communion of the covenant and having thee in the covenant as the good one in Jesus Christ by the gospel and the Spirit, I delight in thee as the only good, and in nothing else."

This explains the proper, legitimate use and enjoyment of things and persons on earth. We receive them as good gifts from our covenant God, to be used and enjoyed in our covenant life with God and in his service, without setting our hearts on these things and persons. In the language of verse 25, we are not to "desire" them as though they were goods alongside and apart from God. What the psalmist expresses as his experience, the apostle Paul teaches as doctrine in 1 Corinthians 7:29–31:

> But this I say, brethren, the time is short: it remaineth, that both they that have wives be as though they had none; And they that weep, as though they wept not; and they that rejoice, as though they rejoiced not; and they that buy, as though they possessed not; And they that use this world, as not abusing it: for the fashion of this world passeth away.

The apostle's ground for not desiring earthly things is the fleeting, perishing character of all earthly things: "for the fashion of this world passeth away." The ground of the psalmist in Psalm 73 is his experience that God is the only good, although

Psalm 73 also points to the ephemeral nature of all earthly things and relations. When verse 26 declares, "God is...my portion *for ever*," the implication is that we have earthly things for only a very short time.

What folly, what ingratitude, to delight in the earthly gifts rather than in the heavenly Giver!

Does not our sin of not having God as our only delight explain much spiritual weakness and misery in our lives? We have no ardent longing for being with Christ at death or for his coming, because God is not our sole delight in heaven. We become fearful, depressed, or bitter over the loss of this or that thing or person on earth, because earthly life and its pleasures are our chief delight, not God. Certainly this explains why we, like the psalmist, are sometimes envious at the wicked when they prosper, and well nigh despairing when we ourselves are plagued and chastened. The reason that the psalmist's feet were almost gone and his steps had well nigh slipped was that he could not confess, because he was then not living in the consciousness of, the truth expressed in verse 25: "Whom have I in heaven? and with thee I have not desired on earth."

With their confession that God is our only good, verses 25 and 26 are related to the main truth of Psalm 73: God is good to Israel in the earthly circumstances of life, whereas he is not good to the reprobate ungodly. Because God is the only good, the prosperity of the ungodly is not to be envied as though it were a blessing. Because God is the only good, the earthly troubles of the godly are no reason to doubt God's goodness to them, not even if, like Job, we lose all.

God is good to his Israel by giving us himself as the good

one in Jesus Christ. If God should take from us many earthly things, or even all earthly things, even life itself, we have him. Having him, we have all. Having him, we are blessed.

It was the psalmist's sin that in the time of sore trouble his flesh and his heart failed (v. 26). The Authorized Version is mistaken in translating the verb in the present tense, "faileth." Grammatically, the verb is the perfect inflection, which ordinarily must be translated with the past tense, "failed." Neither are the commentators right who explain the verb as a "hypothetical perfect," as though the psalmist considers what might be true, namely, that his flesh and heart might fail. He does not describe his present experience, nor does he reflect on what might be his experience. Rather, he looks back on what was actually the case in the time of his great spiritual struggle, when he envied the prosperity of the wicked and doubted God's goodness to him. His physical powers were spent; his flesh failed. So severe was the struggle in connection with his grievous afflictions that also his heart failed. The heart of a man is his spiritual center. For one who fears God, it is the seat of his relation to God by faith. On his part, the psalmist was at his end spiritually. He was ready to give up on God, ready to abandon his trust in God, ready to conclude, "Verily I have cleansed my heart in vain, and washed my hands in innocency" (v. 13).

So serious is the temptation to suppose that God is gracious to the wicked in the earthly circumstances of life! So fearful is the spiritual condition of doubting God's grace in everyday, earthly life, because one has convinced himself that prosperity and ease are grace! So grave is the theological issue of common grace!

God kept the psalmist's heart. He did not allow the psalmist's heart to fail. God himself was the "strength of my heart" (v. 26). The vivid Hebrew has, "rock of my heart, God." That which preserved faltering faith in the heart of the psalmist and strengthened wavering trust in the experience of the psalmist was not deliverance from troubles or bestowal of earthly prosperity and ease. Rather, it was God himself. God was the rock of strength to the doubting, slipping, falling, failing psalmist by means of the truth which he revealed to the psalmist in the sanctuary. This is the truth that the end of the psalmist is glory, to which the troubles lead and which they serve. This is the truth that God is the only good for humans, whether in heaven or on earth. And this is the truth that the end of the prosperous wicked is destruction, to which they slide on the slippery places of their prosperity.

Because God is the only good, the ungodly, who certainly do not have God in Jesus Christ, have nothing, even though they briefly possess earthly prosperity and ease. Lacking God, they lack all good. The gifts without God are not good for them, are not blessings. Their prosperity, which rather than God is their heart's delight and portion, plunges them into destruction.

How can that which is given to the wicked in order to set them in slippery places be blessing (v. 18)? How can that be grace which is used and enjoyed by those who are "far from thee [God]," that is, separated from the God of all grace (v. 27)?

And why do we envy the wicked who lack God, the only good?

CHAPTER FOURTEEN

The Goodness of God's Nearness

*For, lo, they that are far from thee shall perish: thou hast
destroyed all them that go a-whoring from thee.
But it is good for me to draw near to God: I have put my trust
in the Lord God, that I may declare all thy works* (Ps. 73:27, 28).

THE concluding verses of
Psalm 73, verses 27 and 28, give the ground, not of anything
in the immediately preceding context, but of the main themes
of the entire psalm. The main theme is the affirmation with
which the psalm begins: "Truly God is good to Israel." Of this
vital truth, verses 27 and 28 declare the ground: *"For...it is
good for me to draw near to God."* The close relation of the
concluding verses to the opening verse of the psalm is indicated by the fact that the same word, "good," used in verse 1
reappears in the concluding verses.

The secondary theme of Psalm 73 is the denial that God is
good to the ungodly—good in the sense of favoring them and
blessing them in the earthly circumstances of their lives. This
secondary, but fundamental, theme is very definitely implied in

the affirmation of verse 1, that God is good to Israel. This secondary theme is argued explicitly in verses 17–22. Verse 27 gives the ground of this secondary theme: *"For,* lo, they that are far from thee shall perish: thou hast destroyed all them that go a-whoring from thee."

The verses with which Psalm 73 ends gather up the great truths of the gospel taught in the psalm, and with which the psalmist struggled, and express these truths in a fitting, ringing conclusion. To be far from God in everyday, earthly life, as the wicked certainly are, regardless of their prosperity, is not to be blessed, but to be cursed. The nearness of God in earthly life, on the other hand, which is surely the privilege of the people of God, is a good to us, is blessedness, regardless of our troubles. The last verse adds the confession that the psalmist, who had struggled with troubles to the point of doubting God's grace and goodness to him, now puts his trust in God, so that he can declare, rather than question, God's works.

Cursed Separation

God is not good to the ungodly who go on impenitently in their wickedness to the end. God is not good to them in their everyday, earthly circumstances. His favor does not rest upon them. He does not bless them. Their prosperity, their trouble-free lives and deaths, and their natural gifts and successes are not due to, nor do they show, the goodness of God's grace and blessing to them. There is nothing about their earthly lives that is enviable in the least.

One thing, and one thing only, about their earthly lives matters: They are far from God. This is what we God-fearing people must notice. This is what must control a theology of the earthly lives of the ungodly. What matters is not that they have wealth, that they are healthy, that the rain and sunshine produce bumper crops for them, or that they write beautiful symphonies, but that they are far from God.

They are far from God spiritually. They are far from him with their unregenerated, unbelieving hearts, with their minds that never think of him in love and adoration, with their wills that do not desire his glory, with their bodies that serve self and the devil. They are far from God with regard to right worship of him, with regard to confession of the truth, with regard to holiness of life.

Indeed, they are separated from God. They are not separated from God regarding their existence, whether in time or in eternity. They might wish that they were! For God sets them on slippery places, God casts them down to destruction, and God terrifies them to death forever. But they are separated from him regarding blessing and favor. They are separated from God with regard to everything that is good for a human being. For God is the good for us men and women, and they are far off.

That they are far from God is not simply their misfortune. It is also their guilt. They are far from God, because they have gone "a-whoring" from him. Men and women *may* not be far from God. They are required to be near to God. God made man to be his friend and servant. Every man and woman ought to be near God, under God, and for God. All ought to live depending on God, worshiping God, serving God, and praising God. That these wicked people are far from God is their act of rebellion, of unfaithfulness, and of dishonoring God, as a woman who plays the whore, whether by an "affair" or by divorce and remarriage, rebels against, is unfaithful to, and dishonors her lawful husband. The human race went "a-whoring" from God in the disobedience of Adam. The psalmist has in view the wicked in the sphere of the covenant who, like Esau, despise the covenant, its life, and its God, but prosper in the world.

They shall perish. This is all that is, can be, or ought to be said about them. This is all that the inspired word of God says about them: "Lo, they that are far from thee shall perish" (v. 27). It is not said about them, nor ought it to be said about them, that they are the objects of divine favor for a little while and are blessed by God throughout their earthly lives. The word does not say, "Lo, they that are far from thee are the objects of Thy grace." The word does not even say, "Lo, they that are far from thee, although they shall perish one day, for the time being are blessed."

Are they far from God? Is he or she (and the second part of verse 27 in the Hebrew original is singular, not plural, individual, not general: "every one who goes a-whoring") someone who has left God for idols? He or she shall perish. He or she shall perish in the destruction described in verses 18–20. This is what the true church must preach. This is what every Christian must testify.

Indeed, every one who goes "a-whoring" from God is already perishing in the prosperous circumstances of his everyday, earthly life. The inflection of the Hebrew verb (grammatically, the imperfect inflection) permits this translation: "every one who is far from thee *is continuously perishing.*" This is the instruction of verses 18–20: those who are far from God are sliding to hell on slippery places during their earthly lives. And this is the forceful teaching of the second part of verse 27: "Thou *hast* destroyed all them that go a-whoring from thee." They perish, do the ungodly wicked, not simply because foolishly they go on in their wickedness to their death, but because God actively destroys them: "*Thou* hast destroyed... them." This is not favor, but wrath. This is not blessing, but curse. But God's destruction of them is not only a future act. It is a reality already during their prosperous earthly lives: "Thou *hast* destroyed ...them." God has destroyed them inasmuch as he has decreed their destruction in the decree of reprobation. God has destroyed them inasmuch as he accomplishes their destruction every moment of their prosperous, godless lives, by setting them in slippery places. Therefore, he has also destroyed them inasmuch as their destruction is certain.

Shall we envy the foolish? Shall we teach the churches to envy the wicked by the doctrine of a common grace of God? Shall we say that those who are far from God because, like whores, they treacherously forsake him are blessed in their treachery and infidelity? Shall we proclaim that being far from God is good?

Verse 27 expresses a truth that is as firm and sure as the great affirmation of verse 1: "Truly they who are far from God perish under God's wrath."

Blessed Nearness

Only to those who are Israel is God good, for the nearness of God is good for man. Literally, verse 28 reads, in the opening words: "But as for me, the nearness of God to me is good." The issue raised in verse 1 was, "Is God good to Israel in earthly life in view of the troubles God's people suffer?" The resounding answer of the psalm in verse 1 is yes. The reason, according to verse 28, is that the nearness of God is good. Having the nearness of God, as Israel certainly does, Israel has God's goodness. The nearness of God is his communion with Israel in the covenant, according to the covenant promise, "I will be your God, and you will be my people." It is the nearness of love. It is the nearness of a father to his dear children and of a husband to his beloved wife. It is such a nearness that by his Word and Spirit God unites all who are Israel to himself in Christ as living members of his body. In this nearness, they have God and his goodness of grace and salvation in Jesus Christ. Although they draw near to God—and they should—he drew near to them first, and always does draw near to them. The "nearness of God" is both friendship with God and the friendship that he initiates in his sovereignty.

The psalmist expresses his personal enjoyment of this goodness of God: "the nearness of God is good *for me.*" By great struggle, he has come at the end to the personal experience of the truth expressed in verse 1: "Truly God is good to Israel."

This does not mean the end of earthly troubles. The rule for the life on earth both of God's church and of the individual child of God is, "through present suffering to final glory." The psalmist will be plagued and chastened right up to the moment God takes him to glory. Now there is shame; the glory comes afterward. The circumstances of the psalmist's earthly life have not changed, nor does he expect them to change. The change is in the psalmist's attitude toward and response to the troubles. Formerly, when he separated his earthly troubles from their end, he resented the troubles as mere evils, even tokens of God's disfavor, and responded to them with the doubt of unbelief. Now, looking to their end in his glory, he receives them patiently and responds to them with the confidence of faith: "I have put my trust in the Lord GOD."

Refuge in the Storms

For the first time, the covenant name of God occurs in the psalm. "God" in the translation of the Authorized Version is in the Hebrew original the name *Jehovah.* This name of covenant faithfulness, fulfilled in the New Testament in the name *Jesus,* is added to the name of sovereign power, *Adonai,* that is, Lord. With regard to all the troubles of earthly life, the psalmist puts his trust in the God of the covenant. In his covenant with the psalmist as a member of Israel, God has promised to be good to the psalmist, not only regarding spiritual life and a future heaven, but also regarding earthly life with all its circumstances here and now. This God can be relied on. He is faithful. In addition, he is mighty to accomplish his promise. He governs health and sickness, prosperity and adversity, success and failure, physical life and physical death. He is Lord of earth, as of heaven.

The word translated "trust" refers to making the Lord Jehovah one's refuge. In all the storms of earthly life—the sorrows and disappointments, the loss and shame, the poverty and bereavement, the scorn and persecution—the psalmist makes God his refuge. There will be storms. If there are no storms in the life of the child of God, there is no need of a refuge. If these storms are not violent, there is no need of *God* as a refuge. To the very last verse, Psalm 73 utterly demolishes the notion that divine love and blessing mean earthly prosperity, ease, and success, whether for the true church (Israel) or for the individual child of God (the psalmist). The psalmist makes God his refuge by believing the covenant promise, "I will be your God, and I will do you good." With God as his refuge, the psalmist weathers the storms. He bears the troubles patiently. With God as his refuge, the psalmist lets the storms do their profitable work upon him. The troubles work his glory. With God as his refuge, the psalmist will not again stumble and nearly fall, regardless of the severity of the storm in his own life and regardless of the seeming tranquillity of the ungodly. God is the "rock of my heart" (v. 26).

Declaring God's Works Truthfully

The purpose of the child of God in putting his trust in the Lord Jehovah is "that I may declare all thy works" (v. 28).

Assurance of the goodness of God to us in the circumstances of our earthly lives may not end in our own comfort, precious though this is. It must end in God's praise. This is our purpose when we come to the assurance of his goodness. This is the purpose of God in assuring us of his goodness to us. His works we now declare. These are his works of destroying, by setting them in slippery places, those who forsake him. These are his works of bringing his children, who are clean of heart, to glory by way of troubles.

Let the church declare these works on the basis of the instruction of Psalm 73.

Let every child of God declare these works, having learned them in the sanctuary and in this way having arrived through fierce struggle at the conviction of heart, "Truly God is good to Israel."

Other RFPA Books by the Author

Better to Marry: Sex and Marriage in I Corinthians 6 & 7 (including as an appendix a sermon on "The Remarriage of the `Innocent Party'")

Common Grace Revisited: A Response to Richard J. Mouw's He Shines in All That's Fair (a critical response to the Fuller Seminary president's advocacy of common grace as the power of the Christian's life in the world)

The Covenant of God and the Children of Believers: Sovereign Grace in the Covenant (in part a critique of the root of the heresy of the Federal Vision in the doctrine of a conditional covenant)

Hyper-Calvinism & the Call of the Gospel: An Examination of the "Well-Meant Offer" of the Gospel

Marriage, the Mystery of Christ & the Church: The Covenant-Bond in Scripture and History (a thorough biblical, doctrinal, practical, and historical study of marriage against the dark background of the approval of divorce and remarriage by evangelical and Reformed churches)

Reformed Education: The Christian School as Demand of the Covenant

Trinity and Covenant: God as Holy Family (a fresh examination of the threeness of God triune as the source and pattern of the covenant of grace in Jesus Christ)

Unfolding Covenant History: An Exposition of the Old Testament, vol. 5, *Judges and Ruth* (an exposition of the history of Judges and Ruth in light of its center in the covenant of grace, with abundant, explicit application to the life of the New Testament church and her members)